How to Listen When God Is Speaking

A Guide for Modern-Day Catholics

How to Listen When God Is Speaking

A Guide for Modern-Day Catholics

Fr. Mitch Pacwa, SJ

theWORD
among us®
press

Published by The Word Among Us Press
7115 Guilford Road
Frederick, Maryland 21704
www.wau.org

18 17 16 15 14   7 8 9 10 11

ISBN: 978-1-59325-183-3
eISBN: 978-1-59325-410-0

Imprimi potest: V. Rev. Timothy P. Kesicki, SJ, Provincial
Chicago Province of the Society of Jesus
November 29, 2010

Scripture passages are the author's translations.
Scriptures passages marked "RSV" are taken from the Revised Standard
Version Bible: Catholic Edition, copyright © 1965 and 1966 by the Division
of Christian Education of the National Council of the Churches of Christ in
the USA. All rights reserved. Used with permission.

Excerpts from *The Spiritual Exercises of St. Ignatius,*
translated by Louis J. Puhl, SJ, © 1951 by The Newman Press.
Published by Loyola University Press, Chicago.

Cover design by Faceout Studios.

Made and printed in the United States of America

Library of Congress Cataloging-in-Publication Data

Pacwa, Mitch, 1949-
  How to listen when God is speaking : a guide for modern-day Catholics /
Mitch Pacwa.
     p. cm.
  ISBN 978-1-59325-183-3
  1. Spiritual life—Catholic Church. I. Title.
  BX2350.3.P32 2011
  248.4'82—dc22
                                              2010047260

To my younger sister,
Claudia Woodhouse,
who so loves being younger
than me.

Contents

INTRODUCTION

Hearing God in the Modern World

The modern world is full of technical complexities. Every day we are presented with new and improved technology—and new challenges of learning how to use it. The problems of the world are even more complex. Why do oil prices fluctuate? Will there be enough money for Social Security and Medicare? How do citizens deal with terrorism, drugs, and international conflicts?

With all these complexities, it may seem like a quaint notion to look to our faith for answers. If I cannot even read the manuals for my cell phone or computer, how can I expect to find guidance from the Bible, which was written by people thousands of years ago? Furthermore, why would modern people want to listen to God speaking to them? What sense does this make in the modern world? Many Christians and unbelievers alike think it makes no sense at all. The Bible and a personal relationship with Jesus Christ seem so irrelevant that they dismiss a life of faith entirely. To them it seems that the Church is concerned only with their sexual morality. They prefer to make their own decisions, or at least to experiment with various options until they find what is right for them.

So the decision to listen to God speaking to us is a radical—and life-changing—one. To have such a desire means that we believe that there is a loving God who cares for us and has a plan for our lives. Such a worldview differs from the secular culture in that our reference point is centered on loving and serving God, not on ourselves and what we can attain.

Believers in God do not look to powerful political leaders or rich and popular entertainment figures as their models. Rather, they look to Jesus Christ, not only as the model of their lives, but as the one who has the spiritual power to transform them into a new creation. That was our Father's intention from the very moment of creation. Instead of seeing human existence as an accident, believers accept that God desired to create the world for the sake of all humanity and to call each individual, without exception, to a unique purpose within history. This means that God created my soul and yours in our mothers' wombs to live precisely at the particular moment of history into which we were born. "Now" is the time for the mission God has chosen for each of us to fulfill. The choice to listen to God and do his will is the most noble, fulfilling, and purposeful thing we can do with our lives.

Listening to God in prayer will give us new and deeper insight into the person of Jesus Christ. As we meditate on his life in the gospels, as we understand the ways in which the Old Testament foretold and prefigured him, and as we gain insight into the meaning of Christ in the letters of the apostles, we will come to know Christ better. He will definitely challenge us. His words and actions in the gospels will challenge our instincts to be self-centered or to focus on our own personal pleasure or the acquisition of property and power. He will challenge those habits of sin that we too easily rationalize.

Instead of letting us slip into mediocrity, Jesus Christ commands us to "be perfect as your heavenly Father is perfect"

(Matthew 5:48). Jesus will challenge our compulsive behaviors and ingrained patterns of wrongdoing and sin. We think that we can never change, and then we find that Jesus changes us the way he changed Matthew the tax collector (Matthew 9:9) or healed the blind man (Luke 18:35-43) or even raised Lazarus from the dead (John 11). Meditation on these actions of Jesus Christ can give us hope that he will raise us up from the death of our bad behaviors and give us new life. When we read about the leper who dared to ask Jesus for a healing (Matthew 8:1-4) or about the woman with the hemorrhage who was afraid to ask but who touched the tassel of Christ's garment and was healed (Mark 5:24-34), then we gain courage to ask Jesus to help us too. By listening to the gospel in prayer, we learn to become the woman who washed Jesus' feet with her tears and dried them with her hair; her great love saved her and her faith freed her from her sins (Luke 7:36-50). Learning to listen to these and other Scripture passages will change our lives into something far better than we could ever imagine—even better than the fantasies we entertain when we buy a lottery ticket and hope to win millions!

Yet listening to God is not as simple as listening to our MP3 players or cell phones. How do we even learn to listen to God? How does someone know whether God is speaking or whether they are hearing a little voice in their own heads? What is discernment of God's will? What are the basic principles of discernment? What are the goals and purposes of listening to God in the modern world? These are some of the questions this book seeks to answer.

Jesus taught on many different levels to the people of his time. He traveled throughout Galilee proclaiming, "Repent and believe for the kingdom of God has come near" (Mark 1:15). Then he called disciples—among them the disciples of John the Baptist (John 1:29-51) and some fishermen at the Sea of Galilee (Matthew 4:18-22)—to form a small group to follow him more closely throughout his earthly ministry. To these disciples he would address the Sermon on the Mount, although a large crowd also gathered around to hear him (Matthew 5:1-2). Throughout his public ministry, crowds listened to him teach in parables, yet he would explain privately to the smaller circle of disciples both the reason for speaking in parables (Matthew 13:10-17, 34-36) and the parables' interpretations (13:16-23, 36-43). The crowds were taught on one level, but deeper explanations and more profound teachings were given to the twelve disciples (John 13–17). Jesus' disciples learned to listen to this wisdom and then shared it with the world.

Today Jesus calls each one of us into that inner circle. He wants to share with us his profound wisdom and his love so that we, too, can share it with a needy world. Let's discover how we can become listeners like Jesus' disciples so that we can hear God in the modern world today, in whatever place or circumstance we find ourselves.

CHAPTER 1

FIRST THINGS FIRST

Affirming What We Believe

We can't listen to God unless we agree with some very basic beliefs about him. First, we must believe that God *exists*. Second, we must believe that God *is knowable to human beings*. And third, we must believe that God *wants humans to know him*.

These principles summarize the most fundamental beliefs of the large group of people who claim to listen to God and who demonstrate it in the way they live. The lives of such people are characterized by genuine love and care, responsible commitment, and a peacefulness that attracts others to them.

One of the reasons why it may be difficult to hear God in the modern world is that we often hear people in our secular culture who disagree with these basic principles. We may hear that it's too difficult to listen to God, that it's not worth the effort, or even that it is a fool's errand—since God does not exist. Despite these trends, however, most Americans do profess a belief in God and are at least open to, if not actively pursuing, personal contact with him.

Underlying these three fundamental beliefs are some assumptions. Let's explore them further.

God has both acted and spoken to humans throughout the history of a specific people, Israel, which has been recorded in the Bible.

The books that comprise the Bible were written from the late Bronze Age or early Iron Age through the period of the Roman Empire. They have tremendous authority for Christians, setting forth a series of norms for God's relationship with man according to which all words and deeds about God are to be measured. Furthermore, the revelation by God occurs in a real historical sequence, wherein the various characters can often be verified by extrabiblical historical writings, monuments, and inscriptions from Egypt to Babylon and beyond, spanning the entire period of revelation. This means that God did not speak through myths but in real history. This basic principle of the Christian revelation leads believers to assume that God will speak to them within the real history of their own lives. Although the Bible is the completed public revelation that still sets the norm for the experience of God, people continue to find him, experience him, and know him within the real world in which they live.

Not only has God created everything that exists, but he creates each creature as good. No creature has been created as something evil, not even Satan.

First, note in Genesis 1 that God spoke each creature into existence: "Let there be light. . . . Let there be a firmament. . . . Let the waters be gathered and the dry land appear. . . . Let the earth put forth vegetation. . . . Let there be lights in the firmament. . . . Let the waters bring forth creatures. . . . Let the earth bring forth creatures." After each of these creative words, God "saw that it was good." Not only is the God-proclaimed goodness of creation a key theme in Genesis 1, but it appears throughout the Scriptures

For instance, Psalm 148 summons not only the angels but also the sun, moon, heavens, mountains, trees, wild and tame animals, birds, reptiles, and all humans to praise the Lord. In fact, it roughly follows the order and list of creation in Genesis 1. The Book of Daniel includes a hymn of the three young men in the fiery furnace, who summon the same creatures to "bless the Lord, praise and exalt him forever!" (see Daniel 3:56-88). Psalm 104 also takes great delight in all aspects of creation.

Of all the creatures God made, human beings are the only creatures made in the image and likeness of God.

On the sixth day of creation, after God has made the land animals and called them "good," a distinctive process of creation takes place. Instead of the usual phrase "let there be," God's decision to create man begins like this: "Let us make man in our image and likeness, according to our likeness. They will rule over the fish of the sea and the birds of the heavens and the beasts on the whole earth and over all the creeping animals that creep on the earth" (Genesis 1:26). No other creature is made in God's image and likeness, and no other animal is summoned to rule over the others. Not even the lion is designated as the king of the beasts, but man is. Note the use of the plural: "Let us make . . . in our image . . . and . . . our likeness." Most modern scholars identify this as the royal plural, which was used by kings to refer to themselves as individuals who represented the whole nation. However, the Fathers of the Church read in this a hint that pointed toward Jesus Christ's later revelation that the one God is three Persons.

Genesis 1:27 adds another distinctive element to the creation of man. Instead of verbs meaning "make," "fashion," or "form," the verse returns to the distinctive verb used in verse one: "God created the man in his image, according to his likeness." Throughout the Bible, only God is the subject of the verb "create." By using this verb, the text emphasizes that the creation of man is a particularly divine act, which only God could accomplish. However, unlike any other creature, the man is created in God's image and likeness. While God blessed the animals so that they could multiply and be fruitful, God extends the blessing of man in 1:28 to include rule and dominion of all the

> Unlike any other creature, the man is created in God's image and likeness.

other animals. The highlight of creation is reached with human beings. Therefore, God does not merely see that it is good but that it is *very* good (1:31).

What does it mean to be made in God's image and likeness? From the text itself, one can readily conclude that humans share in a rule over creatures, similar to God's power to rule over them. Theologians later asked, "What is the distinctive element in man that makes such rule possible?" The answer of St. Thomas Aquinas and most theologians after him is that we humans can know things, reason, and make choices. Because we have reason, knowledge, and free will, we are not only like God, who possesses these qualities infinitely, but we can master even the animals, which are far stronger than we are.

Community is a way for humans to live in the image and likeness of God.

Another way in which we are like God is that we are social. Humans need community in order to live. Children who are abandoned by their families usually die. We also need community in order to allow our distinctive human gifts and qualities to flourish; people learn language, skills, and knowledge from each other, and cooperation within and among communities makes complex civilization possible. Communities characterized by freely given love, as in families and friendships, exhilarate those who love, while the lack of community debilitates and depresses—or worse, causes despair and destruction of life.

Jesus revealed many aspects of the Blessed Trinity to us, including the mystery that self-giving love is the truth of the Trinity. At the Last Supper, he promised that the Holy Spirit of truth would guide his disciples, which is an important insight for the Church (John 16:13). To explain the importance of this teaching, he offered one of the most profound insights into the inner life of the Trinity: "He will glorify me because he has received that which is mine and he will announce it to you. All that the Father has is mine. Because of this I said he receives what is mine and announces it to you" (John 16:14-15). This teaching shows that each Person of the Trinity gives the infinity of what he has to the other Persons of the Trinity, and each one totally and freely receives what the other Persons give; they never hold back anything from the others. In fact, without Christ's profound insight into the inner life of self-giving in the Trinity, St. John could never have written that "God is love" (1 John 4:8). Without Persons who love and are loved, God could not be love itself. Even more amazing, Jesus informed his disciples that they would share in these gifts too.

Since one key characteristic of the Trinity is complete self-giving and total acceptance of the gift of the others, such love in community is an essential component of human existence. That is why God says in Genesis 2:18, "It is not good for the man to be alone; I will make a suitable partner for him." At first, God almost seems to be joking with the man by presenting each of the birds and wild animals. As helpful as horses and elephants might be, none of them are suitable partners, particularly since man was created to rule and dominate the animals. Only when God fashions the woman does the man have a suitable partner. Not only is she a human being with the same gifts of reason and will, but she is able to bond with the man and become one with him. Furthermore, their union makes possible an increase of human

> Human community and self-giving love are key ways for human beings to demonstrate that they are made in God's image and likeness.

community and an expansion of love as they bring forth new life in their children. Human community and self-giving love are key ways for human beings to demonstrate that they are made in God's image and likeness, and as such prove that they are very good, as God declares in Genesis 1:31.

Human beings share in God's ability to know choices and to have the free will to make them.

The most basic choice needs to be an acceptance of God on his terms. This is a decision to love God as he wants, which means with our whole hearts, minds, and souls (Deuteronomy 6:5). Furthermore, if the image and likeness of God mean we are called to an interpersonal communion of love, not only with God, but with other people, then we must choose to accept the other persons in our lives and give ourselves to them in love. This, like the love of God, involves a variety of spiritual and moral choices that the animals never have—or get—to make.

Let us consider the nature of these choices. They fall into two main categories. The first category is a choice between a moral good versus a moral evil. Do I help save an injured person, or do I walk away and callously ignore the situation? The second category is a choice between two things that are morally good. Do I accept a vocation to marriage, or do I choose to become celibate for the kingdom of God? Making such choices is part of the glory of being human.

However, choosing evil over good can turn life into a horror— a murderer, for example, might be wracked with guilt or end up on death row. On the other hand, choosing a lesser good over a greater good might make life less satisfying, as in the case of the intelligent person who turns away from the hard work of an education in order to have an easier life. But before we can discuss the choices between good and evil, we need to understand what evil means.

Evil is not something inherent in any creature. Rather, the good for which the creature was made has in some way been thwarted. This is especially true when another creature with a reasonable mind and free will chooses to use creatures for purposes other than those for which God created them.

Modern people fall into a number of mental traps when it comes to evil, just as the ancients did. For example, is evil a reality or power of its own, or is it just that certain actions and behaviors are considered evil by society? Some researchers from the twentieth century argued that societal norms and morality regarding human sexuality were social constructs and not in themselves inherently evil. Unfortunately, their work influenced many people, allowing them to construct a moral norm that could justify their own misbehavior and sin.

Another trap regarding the nature of good and evil is to value the spiritual life so highly that the material world and all contact with it are considered inherently evil. This was the belief of many groups throughout history, beginning with the Gnostics of the second through fourth centuries and continuing even among some New Age believers today. The two main forms of this tradition take opposite attitudes toward the daily fact of living in the material world. Some become extreme ascetics, trying to avoid as much contact as possible with the material world. Others treat the material world as being of no consequence; therefore, they give themselves permission to commit any act, particularly in regard to sexual license, because the body does not matter at all.

Christians and Jews take a realistic view of evil. It is neither a social construct nor is it inherently tied to the material world, which they believe to be a good thing because God has created it. Rather, evil becomes possible when human beings decide to use the good things that God created in ways that are not truly part of their purpose.

> Evil becomes possible when human beings decide to use the good things that God created in ways that are not truly part of their purpose.

To demonstrate this point, let's examine some of the most popular vices. Alcohol has certain benefits for human beings. Many people who live very long lives report that they have a habit of consuming about one ounce of alcohol a day. However, drinking in excess shortens life considerably and has very negative effects on the alcohol abuser long before death occurs. Sexuality is a necessary good, without which mammals, including human beings, could not exist. It is one of the joys of marriage and brings forth children, who give their parents tremendous happiness. However, misuse of sexuality leads not only to the present pandemic of sexually transmitted diseases but also to the heartbreaks associated with broken relationships, single-parent children, abortion, and other social, psychological, and spiritual devastation. None of these abuses mean that sexuality is evil; it is the experience of sexuality apart from its purpose that causes these kinds of problems.

The Starting Point

Pursuing moral virtue and shunning vice is merely the first—though necessary—step in listening to God. Christians believe that God, who is the source of all that is good, desires good for every single creature he has made. Recognizing his purposes and goals for creation opens the human mind and imagination to incredible wonders. This is true not only for physical nature but for human nature as well. God's purposes for us are that we live in a way that accurately and beautifully reflects his image and that we live with him forever in heaven. Therefore, listening to God's commandments so as to obey them is a starting point on any spiritual journey.

Of course, obeying God's laws is easier said than done. Human beings truly want good things, but their ability to recognize true good and their desires for it are disordered. Often people want too much of certain good things (for example, dessert) or too little of others (for example, exercise).

Being moderate in our appetites is generally a good approach, but it is not the main goal of our moral behavior. Moral questions go far beyond simple moderation. The most serious moral issues arise when the good elements of human relationships that God desires for us become warped. For instance, maintaining one's dignity is a good. However, destroying another person's reputation in order to make oneself appear good is a serious sin—no matter whether the information is true or false.

Sometimes we want good things but our timing for them is bad—either before it is good to have them or after the best time to have them. Certain apparent goods end up becoming the bitter green fruit when they are taken prematurely or the rotten fruit if they are acquired too late.

God speaks to us in his commandments about a wide variety of moral issues. His goal with these commandments is to direct us in achieving the purpose for which he created us. The first three commandments guide us in loving God and serving him, the only

> Keeping all of the commandments helps us achieve personal integrity so that we can live with ourselves in peace and acceptance.

God, with the proper love and respect that is his due. The other seven commandments help us live in harmony with our fellow human beings, with whom we are to experience self-giving love and communion. At the same time, keeping all of the commandments helps us achieve personal integrity so that we can live with ourselves in peace and acceptance.

We need to apply ourselves to letting the commandments guide our lives, particularly in this present period of history, which is characterized by radical individualism and relativism. Contemporary culture tries to portray the ability of each individual to make up his own mind as a higher good than that of obeying any commandments, including God's. Our fallen and sinful human tendencies often lead us to pursue those relativistic choices, making them seem most natural. Often it is only in the bitter aftermath of our actions—the increase of crime, violence, terrorism, family breakdown, and heartbreak—that we learn that

God was right all along. Nonetheless, if the bitter or rotten fruit does not kill us, then we have a chance to learn from our mistakes and correct them. This is the beginning of repentance and listening to God.

Christians who mature in their faith life are aware that God has been very patient with them as they gradually learned how wrong and offensive sin is. Those who allow God's grace to mature their faith recognize important parallels to the ancient people of the Bible. When we study the Bible and observe the growth and development of those whom God called to be his own special people, we can also hope for spiritual maturity to persevere in the life of faith and prayer as the ancients did. King David was a good example of this: He repented profoundly of his sin of adultery with Bathsheba and the murder of Bathsheba's husband, Uriah, and composed the most moving psalm of repentance of all the psalms, Psalm 51, which has been prayed by millions of sinners to this day.

God continues to accommodate himself to the fears, lack of faith, and even sin of modern believers, but only so as to take them to new levels of faith and holiness. In fact, God's fidelity evokes amazement and wonder when it becomes clear that he loves immature, weak, and sinful people unconditionally and that he helps or even impels them to grow in the spiritual life.

Questions for Reflection and Discussion

1. Do you expect God to speak to you within the real history of your life? Why or why not? How would such an expectation improve your listening time with God?

2. Why do you think God made us to live in community? What happens to us when we lack a supportive community?

3. Do you remember a time when you consciously made a decision to love and serve God? If so, what made you realize that you even had a choice? If not, how can making that conscious decision help you to grow in your faith life?

4. How does the Christian perspective on evil help you to understand the evil you witness in the world today?

5. How do you view God's commandments? Do you see them as a way to a more abundant life? Why or why not? How committed are you to obeying them?

CHAPTER 2

MAKING THE COMMITMENT

Loving God above All Things

In the first chapter, I dealt with some foundational beliefs about God that we must hold if we are going to try to listen to him. Since modern culture has shifted away from a faith-based perspective to a more secular view of life, it was necessary to make these principles explicit. This chapter will consider another set of principles for listening to God, which are objective in nature but which the modern world often finds difficult to accept. In order to listen to God, we need to do the following:

- Make a commitment to God ahead of all other commitments.
- Commit ourselves to getting to heaven and avoiding hell.
- Be willing and committed to accepting God's revelation on his terms rather than our own.

A second set of principles is more subjective in nature and will be treated in the next chapter.

Discerning the will of God in our lives and in the situations in which we live is a very crucial element of being a Christian. Along with other gifts of the Holy Spirit, which include speaking in tongues, prophecy, miracles, and healing, St. Paul lists the ability to discern spirits (1 Corinthians 12:8-10). So we begin by recognizing that discernment is a gift that God pours out on us, flowing from the presence of God within us. *God the Holy Spirit makes discernment possible.* What we discern is the distinction between that which comes from God and that which is not from God, or is even contrary to him, which over the centuries has often been recognized as the world, the flesh, and the devil. In this case, the "world" is not that which God created, which is good, but those things of the world that can lead us astray. Similarly, God created humans as good; the "flesh" refers to our wounded nature, which can lead us away from God.

People who have eaten sugar and butter are disappointed with the lack of authenticity of saccharine and margarine. Similarly, those who have been touched by God's goodness are aware that the rest of their experience is true and good only insofar as it is like God or fulfills the purposes he sets out for those things. We need God as our counterpoint to the world, the flesh, and the devil in order to discern what is of God and what is not. For this reason, we start off assuming and believing that it is the presence of the Holy Spirit within us that makes discernment possible.

Is God First in My Life?

In order to be able to discern the will of God, we have to examine what we expect out of life, that is, our most basic values. *The first and most important principle for being able to discern the will of God from other influences is to decide that I want to please God more than anything else in the world.* This issue comes down to a basic choice offered by Jesus Christ to each person: Will you love God with your whole mind, heart, soul, and strength, and love your neighbor as yourself? Until we can say yes to his request, we cannot even begin to discern the will of God. A decision to love God completely frees us to seek his will, no matter what it takes. If I don't desire to please God, I will be not merely incapable but even uninterested in discerning his will.

Even after we have decided to love God with our whole selves, we may encounter difficulties in obeying his commandments, let alone discerning among the various good things God calls us to do. Why do we fail to keep the good intentions we make to God?

> Being committed to God's will calls for integration of each and every aspect of one's life into a unified whole.

One difficulty in giving ourselves completely to God is that we humans tend to place different aspects of our lives into individual and unconnected compartments. We make compartments for God, for the Church, for our career, for politics, for family, and for fun. That makes it easier to rationalize our actions. We can have our "fun" on Saturday night by indulging in immoral behavior and separate it from our time with God on Sunday. Or we can accept a promotion at work because it means more prestige or money, even though it may prevent us from carrying out our obligations to our family.

Being committed to God's will calls for integration of each and every aspect of one's life into a unified whole. How do I

put God first and integrate him into all the aspects of my life—
my moral life, my political life, my sexual life, my family life?
How do I allow God to set the priorities in my life and determine what is most important? We can bring God into each and
every component of our lives through our prayer and reflection.
The Lord God is very interested in our family life: How do we
talk to the other people in the family? God is very interested in
our finances: How well do we work for our money? How well
do we reward co-workers or employees? How do we treat company property? God is interested in our sexuality, particularly
the areas we never mention to anyone else, or at least to very
few. These are the areas in which we can seek God's will and
take action to live it out.

PURSUING ETERNAL LIFE IN HEAVEN

After resolving to love God above all things and integrating
his desires for us into all aspects of our lives, our next goal is to
avoid eternity in hell and to pursue eternal life in heaven. That
may be so obvious that it sounds strange to have to say it aloud,
but we need to say it.

Fifteen years ago, a young woman sitting next to me on a plane
explained why she had left the Catholic faith and started attending a nondenominational church: "The priest at my parish was
always preaching about hellfire and damnation, and I wanted
something more positive than that." I was shocked. Where was
this priest who preached about hell? The only sermons in which
I had ever heard hell mentioned were my own. Although she later
admitted that the priest did not always preach on this topic, I

began to think how her criticism was a frequent one—from both Catholics and Protestants alike—and how that criticism had led to a dearth of sermons about hell. Then I realized that the only public depictions of hellish conditions come not from the pulpit these days but from the movie theater—Hollywood now charges ten bucks to portray horror, mayhem, and terror.

Even outside the horror movies, some characters on screen will snarl, "I'll see you in hell!" right before shooting their victims. Unfortunately, in real life I have come across a few people who seemed to sincerely want to go to hell. I remember a young man who hated his parents *way* more than he loved God. He hated them so much that he said to me, "I'm going to hell, and I'm taking them with me!" Less extreme than his positive hatred but a more common attitude was reflected by this woman's statement: "I know the things I am doing will bring me to hell, but I do not want to stop doing them. I do not think I can stop, so I will end up in hell, and that's the way it is." Still others flaunt a life of sin with no concern for their eternal future. In fact, they insist that nothing they do is wrong to begin with, no matter how self-centered it is. Because of these attitudes, we would do well to make it clear and explicit: Getting to heaven and avoiding hell is one of our highest priorities during our existence on earth.

Jesus' Warnings about the Consequences of Sin

Many people falsely assume that everyone goes to heaven—movies are made that are even based on this premise. The thinking is that nobody ends up in hell because God is too loving to send anyone there. But who talks about hell most often in the New Testament? Not St. Paul, as some would assume, but Jesus himself. Read the Sermon on the Mount and note how many times Christ warns about ending up in Gehenna. Calling a brother a fool while being angry with him makes one liable to judgment (Matthew 5:22). Failure to make up with an opponent can bring one to a spiritual "prison" until the last penny is paid (5:25-26). Not only adultery but even looking at a woman with lust can drag one down to hell (5:27-30). Furthermore, many of the parables about the kingdom of God in Matthew 13 warn about the possibility of being cast into the fire of judgment: the weeds are burned and the wheat is harvested (13:24-30); the good fish are kept and the bad are thrown away (13:47-50). In the last set of parables in Matthew's Gospel, there is the unfaithful servant whose "severe punishment" in Greek literally means "being cut in two" (24:45-51). The five foolish virgins are left outside the wedding banquet in the darkness because Jesus never knew them (25:1-13). The servant who hid his one talent is cast into the outer darkness for failing to use that talent (25:14-30). The goats who did not help the least of their brethren are sent off to eternal punishment (25:31-46).

In these teachings, Jesus makes it clear that spending eternity in hell is the most serious consequence of any sin that a person can commit. Not public shame, not life imprisonment, not torture, not even the death sentence are worse than damnation. Hell does not permit the fellowship of sinners. The misery of hell does not love company because love of any kind cannot exist there. There are only hatred and disgust with fellow sinners, who have so marred the image and likeness of God that they can find nothing in themselves or in one another that is lovely enough to love.

The community for which man was created is inherently impossible in hell because of sin's lonely individualism.

How does thinking about hell help me to be a better person? Is it not possible that making avoidance of hell the central point of evangelization can make a Christian morbid? After all, have not many Christians so focused on hellfire and damnation that they drove many decent people away? Well, fear of hell has certainly been useful to me, particularly in those times in my life that I avoided certain sins not because I was virtuous but just because I didn't want to go to hell. That's not the best motive, but it works just fine sometimes. I'll start off with that in the hope that someday I will see the real advantage to the virtue that is behind God's commandments. In fact, if fear of hell were the only motive preventing a would-be murderer from committing the deed, I could live with that—and so would the victims!

While fear of hell is not a bad motive to help us avoid sin, it is still not enough to sustain a life of virtue and joy. The reason is that the fear and avoidance of something negative, like hell, will not sustain our motivation to pursue the things we *do* want. We end up reacting passively to experiences rather than striving to achieve these goals. This helps explain the temptation of the third servant who received one talent but simply hid it out of fear of losing it. He ended up condemned and cast into the outer darkness precisely because of his cowardice (Matthew 25:24-30). Often an avoidance of evil or a fear of condemnation and failure leads to an overbearing and harshly judgmental approach to self and to others. How many people so fear negative consequences that they cannot see the joy of doing God's will or the peace of practicing virtue? Such people are the model for the negative portrayal of religious hypocrites so often depicted in the popular media.

People also need a strong positive desire for something good and beautiful. Human beings are created in God's image and likeness, so they have an innate urge toward his wonder and the adorable qualities that are his. Only one eternal destination can

> People also need a strong positive desire for something good and beautiful.

offer people fellowship with God and true communion with the people we love and who love us in return, and that is heaven. And a positive goal, powerfully sought with intense desire, will make it possible to take great risks and engage in the great adventure of faith. Only in this way can we understand the parable of the treasure hidden in a field or the pearl of great price (Matthew 13:44-46). When a person appreciates the tremendous value of the treasure or the pearl, he takes the great risk of selling everything he possesses, trusting that the treasure and the pearl will still be there when he can actually acquire them. The saints have had such a desire for heaven, both for themselves and for others, that they have been willing to travel to foreign and remote lands, endure suffering and persecution, and even be put to death.

Desiring the Wedding Feast

Scripture contains many images of heaven, such as the wondrous descriptions of the joys, beauties, and feasting of heaven in the Book of Revelation. The same parables of the kingdom of God in Matthew 25 allude not just to eternal punishment but also to the rewards of eternal life awaiting those who serve God faithfully. One of the most appealing images of heaven for me is Jesus' description of heaven as the son's wedding feast to which many are called but few are chosen (Matthew 22:1-14). For me, a Polish American, weddings were always fantastic fun. While the church service was solemn and beautiful, the wedding party was loud—two Polka bands had to take turns playing so that the crowd could dance into the early hours of the morning. There were always huge servings of food served family style (since most of the guests were family anyway), and relatives in the hundreds, including my great-grandmother Zosia and twenty or more great aunts and uncles. I remember playing all night with my cousins. Those weddings are still among my favorite memories from my childhood. I could imagine such celebrations going on for all eternity.

Christ's parables and St. John's visions set before us the goal that God wants us to desire: eternal life in joy and light with God, the angels, and the saints. We are taught to look forward to witnessing the infinite mystery and beauty of the Blessed Trinity, but one All Saints' Day I received an insight: Our role in heaven is much more than as an observer. While meditating on the readings of the day, I was trying to imagine the joy of seeing the Father, Son, and Holy Spirit in the full majesty of their love for one another, their complete giving of themselves to each other. That seemed like a wonderful vision, much the way it is a great joy to see parents and babies looking into each other's eyes with a sparkle of joy or a couple obviously in love and taking delight in each other's presence. Then I was given another grace: to imagine the Lord God turning his face toward us in infinite and unconditional love. Not only is the infinite love of the Persons of the Trinity for each other but for us as well! We humans will have the opportunity to share in their loving gaze. This will be like being the child or the lover who is looked at with tender approval and affection— for all eternity. Such a wonder motivates me to strive to be with our Lord in heaven, and that goal is a very basic principle that enables us to discern what God is saying to us in this life until we do reach heaven.

ACCEPTING GOD'S REVELATION ON HIS TERMS

So far we have discussed the first two basic principles: making a commitment to God our first priority and making a commitment to avoid hell and to get to heaven. The third principle is to accept God's revelation on his terms and to let it guide our lives. Keep in mind that biblical revelation spans a wide variety of topics: teachings on the history of Israel, the life of Christ, and the early history of the Church, as well as teachings about God and his nature, law and morality, liturgy, and wisdom for living. A book on Scripture interpretation would be needed to analyze each one of these types of literature, and that is beyond the scope of this book—although such study is very useful and should be pursued. Here we will discuss some of the basic attitudes in accepting God's revelation as a principle for listening to God.

People who have faith believe that God is good. They assume that his revelation is true and therefore worthy of belief. Many other philosophies from the past or present have not been shown worthy of belief—Nazism and Communism, for example.

Christians believe that God's revelation is. In fact, if people had applied the norms of revelation to those other philosophies and rejected them as being against revelation, then many would have been saved, in this world and in the next. But what is it that makes God's word so worthy of belief?

Our starting principles, as stated previously, include faith that God is good and that his whole creation is good from its very beginning. We therefore believe that God's word includes laws and moral teaching that are meant to maintain the order of goodness in the world and to make us into good people. For instance,

> The more deeply one reflects on each of the moral laws, the more wise and intelligent each one appears.

if everyone kept the law "Thou shalt not kill," the whole world would be freer to wander the earth without fear. If everyone followed the law "Thou shalt not commit adultery," family life would be made more firm and secure. "Thou shalt not steal" is another inherent good.

Are any of God's laws detrimental to us? No! In fact, the more deeply one reflects on each of the moral laws, the more wise and intelligent each one appears. In fact, Moses proclaimed this truth to the people of Israel just before they entered the promised land:

> Keep them and do them; for that will be your wisdom and your understanding in the sight of the peoples, who, when they hear all these statutes, will say, "Surely this great nation is a wise and understanding people." (Deuteronomy 4:6)

Jesus established a new level of obedience to God's laws in the Sermon on the Mount, revealing a deeper meaning to each commandment that requires a complete change of heart on our part. He never denied the validity of the moral laws of the Old Testament, but he demanded that his disciples go beyond keeping the exterior behaviors of obeying the law. Jesus taught that not only is murder wrong and against God's commandments, but that it is also wrong to hold grudges, insult others, and be unforgiving (Matthew 5:21-25). He taught that adultery is wrong, but he went beyond simple sexual misbehavior to include even looking at another person with lust (5:27-28). This means that even thinking about another human being as a mere object for one's selfish pleasure is also wrong. Of course, this summons within the very depths of one's heart a profound respect for each and every person's inherent dignity. Jesus said that not only is swearing a false oath wrong, but any form of untruth is unacceptable (5:33-35). This teaching shows the inherent value of the truth in and of itself. Never are facts to be manipulated to serve one's selfish purposes. Note, too, that Jesus did not merely want people to suppress their evil urges; he wanted them to let God thoroughly transform their hearts so that they might be "perfect as your heavenly Father is perfect" (5:48).

These descriptions of the positive benefits of God's law and of Christ's teachings simply present reasons to appreciate their good qualities. It is also important to know that society would benefit from keeping these laws. Individuals may recognize that the deep personal integrity of obeying God's law as Christ teaches it in the Sermon on the Mount is a very admirable ideal. The appreciation of the goodness of law is itself a positive step forward, especially given the experience of many modern people since the cultural upheavals of the 1960s. The consequences of a massive disregard for God's laws are all too evident today: a breakdown of the family, lives ruined by drugs or illicit sex, and widespread abortion, among other things.

The Revelation of Tradition

By accepting the word of God as the truth, we must also accept that Sacred Scripture never teaches believers to look to Scripture alone for revelation. Neither does it ever teach that every doctrine must be proven from the Bible alone. In his very first two epistles, St. Paul wrote that the oral tradition is also God's word. First, he wrote: "Therefore we give thanks to God unceasingly because when you received the word of God from hearing us, you accepted it not as the word of men but as it truly is, the word of God" (1 Thessalonians 2:13). Since this letter was the first book of the New Testament to be written, we must conclude that his oral tradition—prior to writing a single book of the New Testament—is also the word of God. In 2 Thessalonians 2:15, St. Paul further teaches, "Hold on to the traditions which I left you, whether by word or by letter." Based on these texts, the Catholic Church accepts tradition as the word of God. This does not refer to any tradition but only to the apostolic traditions, which were passed on by the apostles to their disciples and preserved by the bishops to our own day. As an example of such a tradition, no book of the Bible tells us what books should go into the Bible. This was an apostolic tradition passed on by the bishops throughout the Christian world.

If the Bible teaches the importance of the traditions of the apostles, then another principle inevitably flows from this: The

Church has an authoritative teaching role in passing on these traditions. St. Paul wrote that the "household of God, that is the church, is the pillar and bulwark of the truth" (1 Timothy 3:15). This confirms the words of Jesus Christ at the Last Supper when he promised to send us the "Spirit of truth, who will lead you into all truth" (John 16:13). Still earlier, as Christ began to move toward Jerusalem in the last months of his public ministry, he accepted Simon's confession of faith ("You are the Christ,

> The Church has an authoritative teaching role in passing on the traditions of the apostles.

the Son of the living God," Matthew 16:16) as a gift of God the Father. Based on the Father's gift of faith to Simon, Jesus changed his name to Peter (*Kepha*, meaning "crag of rock" in Aramaic but transliterated into *Cephas* in Greek—see John 1:42) and promised to build his Church upon this rock. Jesus said the gates of hell would not prevail against the Church. Furthermore, Jesus gave Peter the keys to the kingdom of heaven. Whatever Peter bound on earth would be bound in heaven, and whatever he loosed on earth would be loosed in heaven (Matthew 16:18-19). Jesus later gave this same authority to bind and loose to the other eleven disciples (18:18). This Scripture passage clearly places a tremendous authority into the hands of the Church and her leaders, an authority that is called "the Magisterium" by the Catholic Church.

Such an idea is not popular today, but these and other texts of Scripture teach the authority of the Bible (2 Timothy 3:16), sacred

Tradition (2 Thessalonians 2:15), and the Church (1 Timothy 3:15). These aspects of God's revelation are part of the assumptions of this book, and they should be the assumption of every person who believes that God has inspired the Scriptures.

THE GREAT ADVENTURE

As good as it is to appreciate God's laws as revealed by Scripture and Tradition, every person must still face another set of life-changing questions. The answers will determine one's whole direction of life in this world and in the next. Do I accept these laws as truly given by the good God for my personal benefit and that of the whole world? Or do I see them as merely humanly imposed ideals that I and others can change as we see fit? Do I accept God as the author of absolute laws to which I must conform my life? And most important: Will I commit myself to obeying God and his laws for the rest of my life? Will I reject the temptation to break his law and go against many of my first impulses in order to listen to God's law?

If we answer any of these questions negatively, then we have to recognize up front that we do not want to listen to God. Then this book will have no value. Positive answers to these questions, especially the last one, mean that we are willing to commit ourselves to listening to all that God says about himself and about the nature of being human and of living on this earth.

Anyone who makes the commitment to listen to God is in store for a great new adventure. Accepting God's word as authoritative will include the moral teachings described previously, and obeying them will evoke discipline and, at key moments in life, heroism. Yet God's word includes much more than moral teaching. For instance, the history of salvation as revealed through Israel and the early Church is not only interesting on its own terms; it becomes a mirror that reflects our own lives and God's dealings with each individual and with the whole community of believers. Part of the task of listening to God entails close reading of Scripture and prayerful reflection on it. The believer can expect to hear God speaking to the depths of his or her heart through the words of the Bible.

Listening to God's word will mean developing a whole new and improved attitude toward the world. Believing God's word does not mean rejecting modern science or critical studies of history, literature, psychology, and other fields of study. Rather, by accepting the authority of God in our lives, we will return to these

> Listening to God's word will mean developing a whole new and improved attitude toward the world.

wonderful human endeavors with a perspective that challenges many of the assumptions the so-called "experts" make about life and its meaning. At the same time, as we learn more about science and history, our listening to God's word becomes deeply informed and refined.

For example, many modern Christians are challenged with the scientific theories of evolution and of the Big Bang origin of the universe, as if they cannot coexist with the truth of the Bible. However, the simple presentation of the creation in Genesis 1 is given more flourish and reality when we understand the Big

Bang theory, the speed of light, the pull of gravity, the creation and destruction of stars, and so much more. The biologist who investigates living organisms in depth becomes amazed at the intricate development that automatically happens when a new human being is conceived and a simple fertilized egg becomes a wondrously complex baby. In other words, the sciences reveal glimpses into the magnificence of the world, and for people of faith, further show the infinite goodness of the Lord, who designed wonders that continue to fascinate our best minds.

To summarize, three basic and objective principles are needed for anyone who wants to listen to God speaking in his or her life. First, our commitment to God needs to be ahead of all our other commitments. Second, we commit ourselves to getting to heaven and avoiding hell, a point that demands listening to God correctly. Third, we are committed and willing to accept God's revelation on his terms rather than our own. The next chapter will discuss a second set of principles, subjective in nature, that will help us listen to God by observing how he moves in our souls.

Questions for Reflection and Discussion

1. Examine every area of your life—such as your family life, your work, your moral life, even your recreational activities. What can you say is your most important goal in each of these areas? Do you seek to listen to and please God in every area of your life?

2. Has fear of going to hell ever helped you to avoid a sin? Is it the main reason you avoid sin, or are there other reasons? If so, what are they?

3. How does imagining what heaven is like help you to grow in desire for it? How might the Scriptures help you picture heaven?

4. What are the consequences of disregarding God's laws, both for the individual and society? How have these consequences affected you or your family personally?

5. Why is it so important to obey God's commandments when we are trying to listen to God speaking to us? What can you do when you realize you have failed to obey God?

6. Which commandments do I find it most difficult to obey? Why are these so difficult for me?

CHAPTER 3

THE MOVEMENTS IN
OUR SOULS

*St. Ignatius' Rules for the
Discernment of Spirits*

In the last chapter, we described some basic principles underlying discernment of God's will—committing ourselves to God first, committing ourselves to getting to heaven, and accepting God's revelation on his terms. These basic principles belong on the objective side of the ledger in discernment. Perhaps we can understand them as the bones of a vertebrate animal—they provide the structure. But these bones need flesh, blood, a heart, and a brain. Unlike Dorothy's traveling companions in *The Wizard of Oz*, we already possess them. The question is how do we listen to God speaking to our hearts, minds, and wills? What is the process of discernment of God's will? Interior, personal discernment depends absolutely on those objective first principles, but in our relationship with God, discernment definitely takes a very subjective turn. We move from knowing those extremely important things *about* God to a personal level of *knowing* and *loving* God.

Such a knowledge and love of God occurs within one's prayer life. Prayer includes a communal prayer life in the liturgy, in the sacraments, and in families and prayer groups, as well as a personal prayer life. Prayer is discussed in more depth in later chapters. Here it is important to note that a common aspect of all these types of prayer is the experience of God's peace, a key element of knowing that he is present to us. One aspect of developing spiritually is to learn how to distinguish our compulsive behavior, sins, emotional desires, drives, and inner movements from the peace that comes from God. Familiarity with God's gift of "peace that surpasses understanding" (Philippians 4:7) makes it possible to discern God's leading from our own inclinations, since what is not from God cannot convey a peace that lasts.

At the outset, a few words of warning are appropriate here. We should be careful not to substitute our knowledge of theology for an authentic personal relationship with God. Truly, knowing about God does not necessarily save a soul from sin. In fact, "the demons believe in God, and they tremble" (James 2:19). Some Christians so emphasize their knowledge of God that they fall into various temptations that cause them to be prideful or even arrogant, as St. Paul warns in 1 Corinthians 8:1 ("Knowledge puffs up but love builds up"). This knowledge *about* God must be integrated into the whole of our personal relationship *with* God. Of course, that doesn't mean we should abandon the study of theology or the doctrines of the faith. Some believe that a personal "heart" knowledge of God means that we can dispense with learning about doctrine. Neither option is healthy, because the task of discernment will be a process of integrating all aspects of our person—mind, heart, body, and will—into our relationship with God.

The Lord wants an authentic relationship with us in which we reveal our true personalities to him. He wants us to freely admit who we are, including the character flaws and sinful actions that we would rather keep out of the discussion. At the end of the Sermon on the Mount, Jesus even talks about people who say, "Lord, Lord" and perform mighty deeds in his name but fail to do his Father's will. He will say to them, "Go away, because I never knew you" (Matthew 7:21, 23). Jesus will not be schmoozed by fast-talking, miracle-working wise guys. He desires a personal relationship and not merely nice words *about* a relationship. Such a personal knowl-

> The Lord wants an authentic relationship with us in which we reveal our true personalities to him.

edge based on the truth of our lives is crucial for discerning God's will. Like politics in my hometown of Chicago, it's not what you know but who you know. We need to know God through a rich prayer life, which will be discussed in chapters five and six.

Learning about Interior Discernment

In third grade Sr. Cordelia gave out free tickets to the movies for every student in the class. In fact, Catholic school kids throughout Chicago were offered the tickets to see a movie about a Catholic saint. We talked Mom into driving us to the theater. What made an impression on me then was a big battle at a castle and a brave soldier wounded there. After the fights ended, not much else made sense to me. Ten years later I realized that the movie was about the life of St. Ignatius of Loyola, the founder of my order, the Jesuits. Over the years I have found his story to be so important for understanding the rules for discernment of God's will that I want to pass it on to you.

The battle portrayed in the old movie took place at Pamplona between the French and Spanish in 1521. Ignatius, known then by his Basque name, Inigo, was wounded in the leg by a cannon-ball. He was so admired for his bravery that the victorious French soldiers carried him to his family castle at Loyola. The broken leg had been set poorly, and it healed crookedly with an unsightly bump. He asked the doctors to straighten out the leg (without

> Pay attention to the spiritual movements occurring in your actual life situation.

anesthetics) so that he might look good for the ladies—as being with the ladies was his favorite pastime. But infection set in and nearly killed him until he had a vision of the Blessed Virgin and St. Peter. Still, a year-long process of recuperation left him in bed, bored out of his soldier's mind.

Inigo asked his sister-in-law for some books about battles, knights, and chivalry, but the castle had none. The only two books available were ones about the life of Christ and the lives of the saints. Inigo finally got so bored that he read them. When he wasn't reading, he continued to imagine feats of chivalry and winning great battles, which excited him and made him feel good. Yet after a short while, he would find himself feeling flat and empty. He then went back to reading about Christ and the saints, imagining Christ as a great king and the saints as his knights and ladies of the court. This also made him feel good, but these good feelings and a sense of peace remained with him for a long time afterward. He finally noticed this pattern and decided to give up knighthood, turn to Jesus Christ, and make a pilgrimage. Eventually he founded the Society of Jesus—a task he had never anticipated and an adventure that has changed the history of the world in so many ways. This was also the way he learned about interior discernment of God's will. As a result, he became a great teacher of discernment—both for his contemporaries and for generations ever since.

What can we learn from Inigo? First, begin with your actual life. In Ignatius' case, he was a loyal Catholic who cared more about defending external attacks on the faith than living out its morals and piety. He needed a personal conversion from a sinful life to a virtuous one. This need to pay attention to one's actual circumstances applies to everyone. People come from so many diverse backgrounds and experiences; we don't have to try to make someone else's experiences fit our own life. Simply know yourself and your own real conditions: What has been the pattern of your moral life? What kind of piety are you comfortable with? Do you pray? What do you do in prayer, and what are the subjects of your prayer?

Second, pay attention to the spiritual movements occurring in your actual life situation. Inigo felt movements of peace both when thinking about chivalry and when reading about Christ and the saints, but one peace lasted and the other did not. What movements do you experience? Are there times of great joy and consolation? Do feelings of holiness, emptiness, and desolation come into your life? What do these experiences mean, and how do we know whether God is speaking to us through them? If God is speaking, how can we discern what he is saying? To answer these questions, Inigo wrote some rules for interior discernment.

Ignatius' Rules for the Discernment of Spirits, as they are known, are included in paragraphs 313 to 336 of his famous book, *The Spiritual Exercises*. The purpose of these rules, he says, is to help people understand these diverse interior movements so as to accept the good ones and reject the bad ones (§ 313). This is easier said than done, because people experience so many different spiritual movements that they do not usually think about them or reflect on them. How often do we even identify the various spiritual movements within us? How commonly do we ignore them? Do we ever speak of them to our closest friends? Such awareness that anything spiritual is happening inside us is the first step of discernment.

Having the objective norms of Scripture and Church teaching as our backdrop, we can then begin to evaluate the movements within our souls. What makes them pleasant or unpleasant? Are some of them good or are some of them evil? After discussing the purpose and goal of the rules of discernment, we can examine the actual rules. But first, let's make it clear why these rules can help us in growing closer to God.

Why Are These Rules Important?

In these modern times, the spiritual life is often treated as simply another way to improve your life. According to a number of studies, prayer may lower the risk of heart attack as well as lower blood pressure, so people may turn to prayer or meditation simply to achieve these health benefits. Some want nothing to do with organized religion but desire a spiritual experience so that they can achieve a certain level of peace and comfort in their lives. The assumption underlying these sentiments is that spirituality is an "extra bonus" in life, directed toward personal benefit if the need or inclination is felt by someone.

St. Ignatius Loyola understood the spiritual life as an eternal life-or-death reality. As someone who had been on a path to spiritual death through his desires for military glory and beautiful women, he knew the struggles and dangers of misleading himself spiritually. Once he repented and decided to change his life, he made a pilgrimage to the Shrine of the Blessed Mother at Montserrat and lived a life of penitence, prayer, and seclusion in a cave at nearby Manresa. Though he had decided to embark on the spiritual life, he still experienced great temptations and attacks from the devil in the form of pride, false mortification, and scruples. However, in the process of spiritual growth, he learned the rules for discernment, which he wrote and which have been passed down to us through the ages.

I find St. Ignatius' understanding of the spiritual struggle and even spiritual warfare more true to the experience of the people that I direct and counsel, as well as to my own experience, than some of the current therapy-based views that purposely avoid questions of good and evil. God eagerly desires our souls to turn to him in love and commitment; the enemy of our souls wants to turn us away from God, virtue, and holiness. God is infinitely more intelligent than us, but so is the enemy, though not as wise and smart as God. We all need to be aware of the spiritual war in which our souls are engaged. We can learn how to win the battles against various kinds of temptations. Ignatius' rules for discernment are important tools to alert us to the ways in which any of us might fall into temptation so that we can always be ready with a tactic that moves us toward salvation.

Taking Note of Our Circumstances

In identifying how to recognize the presence of a good spirit or a bad spirit, the first two rules for discernment (§ 314–315 in *The Spiritual Exercises*) take special note of a person's circumstances. Rule one describes the situation of a person who has been committing one mortal sin after another. The tactic typically used by the enemy of our souls is to propose ideas of illusory gratifications or "apparent pleasures" associated with various deeds, "filling their imagination with sensual delights and gratifications."

One very commonly committed sin is missing Mass on Sunday and holy days. When someone has a lukewarm attitude towards this obligation, it is easy to let the eyelids droop on Sunday morning and stay in bed for that extra beauty sleep. If a person misses one Sunday, it is easier to miss the next one or even a long string of Sundays. The person may think thoughts such as these: "What's the use of going to church this week? I missed last Sunday, and I have to go to confession anyway. And isn't it just as good to be loving to other people as to go to church? Maybe I'll take the family for a leisurely breakfast at a restaurant. And wouldn't the family enjoy a special treat of a baseball game?" Ball games and breakfasts out are simple pleasures in themselves, and it is these that come to the foreground in the temptation to keep missing the Sunday obligation to worship God and receive Jesus Christ at Mass.

Another common example of the temptation to commit sin with attendant illusory gratifications and apparent pleasures occurs to people who struggle with pornography and easily succumb to the temptation to visit pornographic Web sites. These visits sometimes trigger the introduction of software into the computer's operating system that automatically routes the computer to other pornographic Web sites, thereby making it even more difficult for the user to end the addiction. A middle-aged man told me, "My computer keeps hooking up with these sites, and I do not feel strong enough to learn how to make it stop." The point St. Ignatius makes in the first rule of discernment is our need to identify such a temptation to illusory pleasure as an enemy spirit. That spirit creates excuses that stem from a person's laziness ("I don't know how to make it stop") in order to mask the desire to keep returning to the pleasure.

> We may not worship golden calves as the Israelites once did, but we certainly make idols of our own pleasures and possessions.

We may not worship golden calves as the Israelites once did, but we certainly make idols of our own pleasures and possessions. We would do well to examine our consciences to detect the idols we set up for ourselves. These temptations must be treated as opponents to be thoroughly defeated.

For people who are committing mortal sin, the good spirit, according to the first rule, uses a contrary tactic: Making use of reason and thought, he "will rouse the sting of conscience and fill them with remorse." This flies in the face of the claims of certain pop psychologists that feelings of guilt must be avoided at all costs. To their thinking, if we deny that our behavior is bad, then we remove the guilt feelings. In contrast, St. Ignatius identifies the pangs of conscience and remorse over evil behavior as a movement of the Holy Spirit. Guilt alerts the conscience to the presence of a moral problem. Precisely because guilt is an unpleasant experience, the person is motivated to take action to remove the guilt. Instead of merely denying that the guilt exists, the person can come to God for true reconciliation, forgiveness, and the request to make a change of behavior toward moral and good action.

Rule two addresses the person who has already decided to improve his or her spiritual life and move from good to better in service of God our Lord. The spiritual movements act in ways contrary to the first kind of person. These people experience the evil spirit trying "to harass with anxiety, to afflict with sadness, to raise obstacles backed by fallacious reasonings that disturb the soul," thus preventing the soul from advancing. Note that the evil spirit has forsaken the temptations to pleasure. Instead, it tries to make a person afraid of pain: "How can you commit yourself to a holy hour before the Blessed Sacrament every week? What about the times when you might miss out on a party or family get-together during your holy hour? How can you sign up for that 2 a.m. slot? You will be too tired to get up at such an hour, and the next day you will be miserable at work because you will be too sleepy."

This evil spirit commonly attacks those recovering from alcohol and drug addictions. The person may have firmly resolved to stop drinking for the rest of his or her life; the hangovers are too painful, and the effects of the drinking on family, friends, and careers are too destructive. However, the idea of never having another drink begins to weigh heavily upon the person: "How can I go on for the rest of my life without having a little drink once in a while? I don't think I can do it!" Life without booze begins to sound meaningless, and the alcoholic is strongly tempted to get drunk just to cope with the loss of booze.

On the other hand, the good spirit tries "to give courage and strength, consolations, tears, inspirations, and peace," making it easy for the person by "removing all obstacles so that the soul goes forward in doing good." In the situation where a person has committed to a holy hour once a week, the good spirit reminds the person of the peace that is felt not only during Eucharistic adoration but for the rest of the day. The whole week seems to go more smoothly, and amazingly, more things get done the next day after a holy hour than on other days. Similarly, the alcoholic realizes that he is not more powerful than booze but that God is. God can help him one day at a time or, if need be, one hour at a time. By breaking down the task of avoiding alcohol into small increments, the alcoholic can take on the struggle for the rest of that single day or hour. Then there is peace with each bit of sobriety. Of course, this principle applies to overcoming any habitual or addictive behavior.

Ignatius' Descriptions of Consolation and Desolation

The next two rules (§316–317) describe the experience of consolation and desolation. Rule three describes the common experiences that are associated with spiritual consolation. The first characteristic of consolation is a prompting to be "inflamed with love of its Creator and Lord." Compare this description to the experience of so many people who speak of "the Man upstairs," with a wary respect for what he might do to you—whether good or bad, reward or punishment. Some people have a certain cultural reverence and fear of God, but they are hardly aflame with love. Only after experiencing God's reciprocal love does a person experience a burning love for God—particularly after a conversion when the person is convicted that God has forgiven his sins that have been confessed honestly and forthrightly. St. Ignatius recognizes that this is a movement of God's good Spirit and not an emotion produced merely by humanly engineered psychological tricks.

A consequence of this love is a change of attitude toward other creatures. Sinful behavior is often characterized by a focus on possessing various things or on the pleasure derived from those things. A person who is experiencing consolation loves these things only in God who created them. For example, a thief might rejoice in a sunset because he can use the darkness to break into someone's house, but the person who is moved by consola-

> Only after experiencing God's reciprocal love does a person experience a burning love for God.

tion cherishes the beauty of the sunset as a reflection of God the Creator. As the cartoon character Ziggy exclaimed while viewing a particularly beautiful sunset, "Author! Author!" Nature is not worshiped in itself, as in paganism, but the Lord of nature is loved. Every creature is appreciated for the beauty that God has bestowed on it, the beauty that Michelangelo displayed in paintings or that Bach set to music.

Another component of consolation is a strong emotional response to the realities of the spiritual life. For instance, tears are shed as a person realizes more poignantly the seriousness of his or her sins. The reality of having offended God, whom one has come to love more deeply, evokes tears of grief. This stands in contrast to those who are still so distant from God that they do not think their sins are bad enough to even need confessing. St. Ignatius experienced a gift of tears so often, particularly when celebrating Mass, that the doctor warned him about damaging his eyesight.

Consolation is experienced with tears of sorrow as a person meditates on the depths of God's love manifested in the sufferings of Christ. How many people watched Mel Gibson's film *The Passion of the Christ* and were moved to tears, particularly when the depictions of Mary's grief at Jesus' crucifixion were interspersed with flashbacks to the child Jesus running into the arms of his mother. Similarly, experiences of joy, such as when a person considers heavenly things or the mysteries of the faith, are movements of the good Spirit.

Increases of faith, hope, and charity are characterized as consolations by Ignatius. A more ready acceptance of the truths of the faith is a sign of consolation. Having greater hope of being with God in heaven is a consolation. Along with these experiences come a stillness in the soul and an interior peace that endure for significant periods of time. In fact, sometimes even people imprisoned and tortured for their faith and facing death experience these things.

I was privileged to meet a Jesuit who had worked in China in the early 1950s. After the Communists took control of the country, he and his Jesuit colleagues were arrested and put in prison, where they were ordered to meditate on their "sins of capitalism" in solitary confinement for hours every day. The Communists hoped to break their will and destroy their minds. However, my friend used that time to recite the words of the Mass to himself, pray the Rosary, and reflect on various passages from Scripture that came to his mind. After several years, he was permitted to receive a package of food his mother had sent him, including hard candy wafers. When he opened the package of candy, he found that she had placed an unconsecrated host in between each wafer. In the "medicine" bottle she had sent him was wine. He used the cap as a chalice, celebrated Mass, the words of which he had repeated over the years, and then broke the host into tiny fragments so that each of the other imprisoned priests could receive Jesus. He remembered this experience more powerfully than the suffering he had undergone, a sign of true consolation in a terrible situation. Of course, the presence of consolation does not eliminate the experience of pain. But the "peace that surpasses understanding" (Philippians 4:7) that the Jesuit priest experienced happened because of his positive and ongoing relationship with God.

In Rule four Ignatius describes desolation as the opposite of consolation. The soul feels turmoil and darkness and an inclination to what is low and earthly. Many disturbances and temptations make the person restless, and this leads to a lack of faith, hope, and charity. The soul feels sluggish, slothful, sad, and separated from God. The spiritual life is tepid or lukewarm and does not bring joy or peace.

How to Behave during Spiritual Desolation

The next rules consider how a person should behave during the experiences of desolation and consolation. Rule five (§ 318) warns against making decisions during times of desolation. If someone has already made a decision before the desolation set in, or made the decision in a time of consolation, then he or she should never change that decision during a time of desolation. Ignatius advises us to treat the desolation as a temptation and hold steady the course of action already chosen. He warns that the bad spirit wants to guide and direct us through desolations, but following the counsel of a bad spirit will never lead to the right decision.

As is typical of Jesuit seminarians, I was assigned to teach high school immediately after completing my philosophy studies. I did not like the idea at all. In fact, I recall feeling as if I had been thrown off a tramp steamer in the middle of the ocean on a dark night: I had no way of knowing whether land was a hundred yards to my left or a thousand miles to my right. In this state of desolation, I had my one and only temptation to leave the Jesuit Order. However, like a pinhole of light in the darkness, I remembered the experience of my long retreat as a novice, when I became convinced that God had called me to be a Jesuit. I could not deny that experience, and remembering it carried me through the desolation associated with that high school assignment. By remaining faithful to my vocation, I learned how to be a teacher precisely from those young men whom I had not wanted to teach. To them, I remain grateful; to God, I remain eternally grateful for reminding me of St. Ignatius' fifth rule of discernment.

Rule six (§ 319) adds to the rule against changing decisions while in the state of desolation. Instead of merely arguing with the desolation, we should take every opportunity to "intensify our activity against" it. We should take time for more prayer, meditation, and especially self-examination. In fact, doing penance is a very useful practice while experiencing desolation.

When I arrived at St. Xavier High School, the principal assigned me to work with a small group of boys who had asked to pray together every day for twenty minutes before classes began. Though wary at first, I came to enjoy meeting with these young men because I knew I had to be more regular about my own personal prayer life before coming to the prayer meeting with the boys. This regular prayer life with a group and in private became the way through which I eventually came to realize that teaching at the high school was part of a larger plan of God: It led me away from some New Age ideas to which I had been clinging and toward a deepening of my Catholic faith.

Doing penance is a very useful practice while experiencing desolation.

In Rule seven (§ 320), Ignatius explains that the person experiencing desolation should consider that the Lord has left him to his natural powers so as to test his strength in resisting temptations. At the same time, he says, the person needs to have faith that God's assistance is always still present, even if he does not clearly perceive that he is being tempted. The person should keep in mind that the graces will not be so filled with positive emotion or "overflowing love," but that the Lord always provides enough grace for overcoming temptation and moving toward eternal salvation.

This situation can be compared to soldiers or athletes who are being pushed beyond their normal routine into an excruciatingly difficult drill. Their bodies and minds strain to a breaking point, and they may even want to quit. Yet only when they are in the midst of a crucial game or when they are caught in life-threatening combat do they realize that their earlier training built their endurance and is now paying off.

Or consider how parents feel when a child gets into very serious trouble. Though they may be distraught, their love for that child carries them—and their child—through the crisis. In the same way, so does God's love and grace continue to be with us in times of desolation and apparent spiritual emptiness. In fact, situations in which our strength is tested make us stronger for the more difficult trials still ahead in our lives.

Rule eight (§ 321) is a reminder of what can encourage us during desolation. First, we must make an effort to hold onto our faith patiently, because patience counteracts the harassments that come from the bad spirit. We should also hunker down and pray more, meditate more, do more penance, and examine our lives more often. Throughout the whole time of desolation, we must keep in mind that it will come to an end and be replaced by consolation.

Imagine the depths of desolation that the Blessed Mother felt on the evening of Good Friday and on Holy Saturday. Most Christians try to enter into these days through the liturgical and hymnic expressions of sorrow, but they would do well to simply try to imagine what the Blessed Virgin Mary might have felt at the death of her child. Of course, those parents who have lost children understand quite readily. Other people may want to remember the loss of a particularly dear and close person as a way to enter into her grief.

Then consider the moment when Mary knew that Jesus was truly raised from the dead. (Next to the Holy Sepulcher in

Jerusalem is a chapel dedicated to Christ meeting his mother, Mary, after the resurrection.) Most of us Christians enter this joy through the exultant hymns on Easter, along with the flowers, the pealing of bells, and the feasting. These all bring our sorrow over the death of Christ to an end; in fact, the more profoundly a Christian enters the grief over the death of Jesus, the more powerful is the joy on Easter. So should Christians consider that the difficulties of a personal desolation will eventually be followed by a proportionate consolation.

Causes of Spiritual Desolation

Rule nine (§ 322) is an explanation of the three main causes for why a person enters into a spiritual desolation. First, some people become tepid in devotion or lazy about doing spiritual exercises or even downright negligent. Of course, it is easy to let the busyness of the day get in the way of doing spiritual exercises such as daily prayer, Mass, or the Rosary. However, when we become so neglectful, we should expect spiritual desolation to come to us. We need to remember that missing our time with God is truly missing out on life's joy, and its omission will contribute to a desolate state in our souls.

The second reason for desolation is that God desires to test us. Though a person may not have done anything wrong, the Lord wants to see how far we will extend ourselves in serving and praising him, even when we do not receive consolations in return for our efforts. This type of testing gives us greater strength, even in the midst of anxiety and spiritual emptiness. This is not unlike the experience of taking tests in school. Even though a student may be well prepared for the test, he or she may feel nervous, anxious, or unsure until the test results come back. Yet while the test may have caused stress for the student, it also motivated him or her to study the material more diligently and learn how to explain it, bringing that knowledge from a passive to an active level. Similarly, the test of spiritual desolation helps the soul better understand and put into action the commitments already made to love and serve the Lord.

> We need to remember that missing our time with God is truly missing out on life's joy.

It does not hurt to remember that Jesus Christ also endured such testing when he fasted for forty days and nights in the desert as well as during his agony in Gethsemane. The same Holy Spirit who had hovered over Jesus while he was being baptized in the Jordan River led him into the desert to be "tempted by the devil" (Matthew 4:1). Clearly, this shows that desolation is not a punishment for sin but is something undergone even by the sinless Son of God. As Hebrews 5:7-8 says:

In the days of his flesh, Jesus offered up prayers and supplications, with loud cries and tears, to him who was able to save him from death, and he was heard for his godly fear. Although he was a Son, he learned obedience through what he suffered.

The third reason for desolation is to make it clear to us that we cannot maintain or create spiritual consolations—including increases of faith, hope, or love or experiences of tears and joy—simply by human means. At times God wants us to become more strongly aware that these consolations are truly gifts of his grace and not merely humanly devised techniques for good spiritual health. This type of desolation reminds us that we are truly in a relationship with the sovereign God and that we cannot manufacture spirituality by our own wits and power. Such experiences can prevent religious and spiritual people from becoming prideful and being tempted to think that they are better than others. Desolation reminds such people that we all have sinned and have fallen short of the glory of God (Romans 3:23). We all depend not on ourselves but on God's mercy, love, and grace.

Preparing for Spiritual Desolation

Rule ten (§ 323) urges those who are experiencing spiritual consolation to prepare for the inevitability of falling into desolation at some later time. After a conversion experience, whether during a retreat or a pilgrimage or through a prayer group, some people seem to think that life will be lived on a spiritual high from that time forward. In fact, certain individuals who are unprepared for the inevitability of desolation try to manufacture positive experiences—grins that stretch their cheeks too widely and enthusiastic talk that does not resonate with others. Perhaps they fear that their witness will not be attractive if they are not permanently happy and joyful, so they falsify good feelings that are not actually present.

Instead of being untrue to the actual highs and lows of the spiritual life, we should prepare ourselves for these ups and downs.

Humility is especially useful, as is an honest awareness of feelings, both positive and negative. Another preparation for desolation while we are in consolation is the development of good habits of piety, prayer, and moral behavior. Healthy, well-trained athletes stick to a solid routine of exercise that will carry them through the times when they are tired or sick. So can a regular spiritual regimen help carry the spiritual life through desolation.

Rule eleven (§ 324) is more specific about the preparations that are needed for changes in spiritual movements. First, keep in mind the ways in which you act during desolation. Be aware of crankiness, impatience, and other unpleasant ways of relating to people when the joys of the spiritual life are not so strong. These memories will hold your spiritual pride in check and can foster a humility that others will appreciate.

Second, during times of desolation, call to mind that God gives sufficient grace to overcome temptations. Though you may feel weak and vulnerable during desolation, God is still the one who is giving the grace that strengthens the weak. St. Paul wrote that he had been given a "thorn in his flesh," which the Lord did not remove even after his three petitions to take it away. In fact, the Lord said to him, "My grace is sufficient for you, for my power is made perfect in weakness" (2 Corinthians 12:9). St. Paul accepted that word and responded, "For the sake of Christ, then, I am content with weaknesses, insults, hardships, persecutions, and calamities; for when I am weak, then I am strong" (12:10). This is the attitude that St. Ignatius is recommending when we are in desolation.

The Tactics of the Evil One

The last three rules for discernment are descriptions of the evil one's tactics, based on examples from St. Ignatius' own culture. Rule twelve (§ 325) describes the enemy of our soul as a certain type of woman (think of Shakespeare's Kate in *Taming of the Shrew* or Bizet's *Carmen*). Such a character wants to argue with and control a man. If the man boldly confronts her, she

> **Call to mind that God gives sufficient grace to overcome temptations.**

backs off, but if he shows any weakness and begins to retreat, she comes at him with "anger, vindictiveness, and rage." Similarly, the enemy of our soul tries to tempt us away from virtue. If we resist with courage and boldly exercise our piety and virtue, the enemy retreats. However, if we show any weakness, vacillation, or interest in the sin, the enemy attacks us with even greater ferocity.

Rule thirteen (§ 326) compares the enemy to a certain type of man (note that Ignatius doesn't use just women in his examples!) who is having a forbidden and clandestine affair with a woman who is not his wife. Such a man insists that his dishonorable advances and romances be kept a secret between him and the lady in question. What he fears most is that she will reveal the secret affair to someone who is responsible, such as her husband or a parent. That revelation would drive him away. However, keeping the seduction a secret helps to keep it going. So also the enemy wants us to keep our temptations and sins a secret from our confessor or spiritual director. So long as we hold the seduction inside of us, we will remain susceptible to it. Simply telling a responsible person about the temptation reduces its power to lure us.

The third tactic of the enemy is described in rule fourteen (§ 327) in military terms. The enemy is like an attacking general who surveys the strongholds of our soul and finds the weakest point. He inspects our theological, cardinal, and moral virtues to see which ones are the weakest. Wherever he finds us vulnerable, he attacks with temptation. Therefore, we should know our weaknesses and work to compensate for them by developing habits of behavior in the corresponding virtues.

St. Ignatius includes a further group of rules of discernment for the Second Week of his Spiritual Exercises (§ 328–336). However, these are better left for a more advanced study. The rules for the First Week of the Exercises are sufficient for the basic type of discernment the average Christian must deal with in the spiritual life. In the next chapter, we'll discuss what we can do to equip ourselves for the spiritual battle ahead.

Questions for Reflection and Discussion

1. How can an awareness of the ongoing spiritual battle going on in your soul help you to reject temptation and avoid sin? Is this awareness currently part of your spiritual life?

2. When has guilt helped you to turn away from sin? Were you able to recognize it as a movement of the Holy Spirit?

3. Think of a time when you experienced either spiritual consolation or desolation. What happened? How did your faith grow as a result of these experiences?

4. Compare your prayer life to an exercise regime. How are you doing? Are you building up strength for the times when you experience desolation?

5. What are your weaknesses and the areas in your life in which you are especially subject to temptation? What corresponding virtues could you develop to help you guard against these weaknesses?

CHAPTER 4

PREPARING OUR HEARTS

Learning Detachment and Trust

St. Ignatius suffered major injuries both in the war against France and the war for his soul. He learned the Rules for the Discernment of Spirits in the school of struggle against sin, deception, and evil spirits, only to discover that this was a fight for God, the truth, and holiness. Like Ignatius the soldier, engaging in this battle requires us to be well equipped. We have to prepare our hearts so that we can really hear the Lord speaking to us.

First and foremost in this struggle, we need an authentic prayer life that deepens our relationship with God and reconciles us to him. We must also have a desire to choose for our lives whatever gives the greater glory to God, which requires that we be "equal-minded"—happy with whatever good option that we discern our Lord most wants for our lives. We also need to trust God so that we can believe that whatever he wants for us has been, like a yoke, especially designed for us alone. He has a vocation or mission that is uniquely ours to fulfill..

PRAYER AND RECONCILIATION

It may be obvious that engagement in this struggle requires us to have a real prayer life, which includes our common prayer in the sacraments and praying together as groups, as well as personal prayer in an ever-closer relationship with Christ. The next two chapters will explore these various types of prayer, but here we can say that the peace we experience in prayer is because of Christ's presence with us, a promise that Jesus made to his disciples:

> "For where two or three are gathered in my name, there am I in the midst of them." (Matthew 18:20)

> "Behold, I am with you always, to the close of the age." (Matthew 28:20)

Attaining peace in prayer requires that we be reconciled with God. One of my favorite sets of icons is in the middle level of the Church of St. Peter in Gallicantu, the Jerusalem church built over the house of the high priest Caiaphas. In the first icon, we see Jesus gazing at Peter, who is standing near a fire as the cock crows. Peter has no halo because he has denied Jesus. The middle icon portrays Peter at the mouth of a cave, weeping bitterly because of his sin; he has a halo simply because he has repented. The third icon shows Jesus standing near a fire, asking Peter three times, "Do you love me?" In this picture the reconciliation of Peter with Jesus is complete; he is restored to the leadership of the apostles and to Christ's own ministry of feeding his sheep. The casual observer might miss that in this icon, his halo shines most brightly. These icons depict the peace of God as already present when we begin in repentance and work through the issues of seeking God's forgiveness.

God's gift of peace may well continue as we learn more about ourselves and the sources of the different sins we commit. We may experience God's peace as we distinguish between our compulsive behaviors, emotional desires, and drives, and the inner movements of our minds and hearts. In fact, many people may be surprised at the peace they experience after a thoroughly honest moral examination of their lives. Oftentimes people are so afraid that if they actually admit to wrongdoing, God will smite them on the spot. On the contrary, honest admission of sin and an acceptance of personal responsibility for the evil deeds may well bring a grace-filled peace, such as St. Peter's halo in the second icon indicates.

> Many people may be surprised at the peace they experience after a thoroughly honest moral examination of their lives.

However, the experience of desolation is not unusual when people ignore, defend, or even embrace those sinful aspects of their lives that separate them from God. God does not want a person to feel comfortable with acts of violence, adultery, lust, stealing, jealousy, or any other degradation of the human person. Quite commonly people who do these things will retreat to a hardened defensiveness of their deeds. They become callous, cynical, and sarcastic, but they do not experience joy and peace. They may even enjoy their sins—for a while. Eventually dissatisfaction sets in and becomes a disconcerting desolation, such as is described in St. Ignatius' fourth rule for the discernment of spirits. If the wrongdoing is not attended to, it may even become self-destructive and destructive of others. A typical example of the destructive quality of sin is when an illicit sexual affair destroys a family or when a drug or alcoholic addiction destroys a person's life.

Familiarity with the peace that God truly offers will determine our ability to separate allurements from the evil spirit and his imitations of God's good work. Like people who know the real taste of maple syrup, butter, or sugar, a deepening prayer life will help us to detect the imitations that are the attractive deceptions posed by the bad spirit.

Of course, people of faith do not need to discern the objective principles we discussed in the first chapter. No one need discern whether or not to commit adultery, steal, murder, or worship other gods. The commandments are not open to personal discernment; you can't ask whether God has given you a special dispensation to commit blasphemy or bear false witness about another person. God has given us those laws. We simply seek to obey them, and we admit responsibility for the times we break them, confessing our sins and seeking God's mercy.

"EQUAL-MINDEDNESS"

However, there are many other areas of life in which I have two or more good options from which to choose. When it comes to dealing with these good, legitimate options, I can either make a decision by the seat of my pants, or I can really seek to determine what God is asking of me. For example, I can look at various job opportunities from different perspectives. I might reason: "Well, there's a lot more money in accounting than in teaching high-school mathematics. Oh, that's a slam dunk—I'll go with the higher salary." Maybe. If we want to do what God wills, then we can be open to any possibility, because God our Lord made everything good, including riches, poverty, or a relatively simple lifestyle. God can work through people with wealth (many saints were kings and queens) or through very poor people (St. Francis of Assisi and many other saints). These various possibilities are good in themselves, and therefore they are ways to become holy and to give glory to the God who made them. How do we choose among these good options?

If God can use everything and everything is good, then an essential starting point of being able to discern God's will is the gift of being "equal-minded." St. Ignatius of Loyola called this gift being "indifferent," but some modern people interpret this term as not caring about the choices. Better is the term "equal-minded," which implies that I am happy to take either this option

> Seeking to give greater glory to God is one of the most important principles of discerning God's will for my life.

or that option. Neither option matters to me except insofar as one gives greater glory to God than the other. Seeking to give greater glory to God is one of the most important principles of discerning God's will for my life.

I learned about equal-mindedness in one of the most important moments of my making a final discernment about becoming a Jesuit. Five months after entering the novitiate, the whole class of first-year novices made the Spiritual Exercises. At the end of the First Week of the four-week exercise, we meditated on the call of Christ the King, in which we first consider the call of a great human king or leader to rectify the wrongs of the world. I thought about President John F. Kennedy, a hero in my early adolescence; St. Ignatius had the emperor Charles V in mind.

Next, we consider how Jesus Christ makes the same kind of call, though for a correction of the world's wrongs on a more profound level than what various political leaders can accomplish. Christ the King is completely up front in having us consider that following him will entail much suffering and deprivation, but the promise of victory over Satan and evil is worth the effort. During a repetition of this meditation, I began to experience a grace of being completely equal-minded in regard to any vocation the Lord might give me. By this grace I was able to say that it did not matter to me whether I got married, lived as a single layman, or became a Jesuit brother or a priest. If I was called to the priesthood, it did not matter whether I belonged to a diocese, the Society of Jesus, or some other order. I was able to say, "Whatever you want, Lord, that's what I want."

This grace of equal-mindedness came only after I had spent the previous ten days of the retreat looking back on my life, examining it honestly, and repenting of my many sins. I came to understand that God loved me as a sinner, and I believed deeply that he forgave me. Based on that knowledge, I became more free from the desires that had led to my sin. I did not need to let those sinful desires control my life. Equal-mindedness became possible because of the joy of knowing God's love for me—even though I had sinned—and of knowing that Christ's death on the cross was the pain he endured to redeem me from sin. Precisely at that point, I felt a tremendous peace about pursuing the call to the Jesuit priesthood, and the peace of that choice or "election" (St. Ignatius' term for it) has been the mainstay of my whole Jesuit vocation for more than forty years. In fact, it has continued to remain a star of light that has guided me when life has become difficult, as I described in the preceding chapter in regard to my temptation to leave the Society during my time as a high school teacher.

Obstacles to Being Equal-Minded

Obstacles to being equal-minded arise when we cling to things and become attached to them, which is the opposite of being equal-minded. We have various reasons for these attachments, most of which depend on the inclinations of our personalities. Some common reasons to be attached to things are fear and pride. We fear other people's negative opinions of us, and we have vague hopes that possessing certain titles, honors, or properties might elevate that opinion. Sometimes pride forms the basis for our attachments: "What will my family say if I am not a success? How will I gain a good reputation among my friends if they cannot see concrete forms of my success?" Whenever I

> My attachments hinder my ability to listen to God.

let fear or pride get in the way, I allow attachments to the good things of this earth to cloud my ability to see and hear the voice of God the Creator. I may not necessarily choose to do evil by pursuing a certain profession or by working to buy a particularly beautiful house in a prestigious neighborhood, but neither will I be able to discern whether this is God's will for me. My attachments hinder my ability to listen to God.

Let me illustrate one of the areas in which I personally learned this truth. When I was a sophomore in high school seminary, I had a job as a busboy. I was trying to earn money to help with my tuition, especially for when I got to the college level of seminary, at which point my parents would not be able to afford to help me financially. To increase my income, I began investing my earnings in the stock market. (I know I was underage, but in Chicago a lot of things become possible if you know people.) I began studying the stock-market reports and researching interesting companies, and eventually I invested my money in a food chain, a mining company, and an aerospace company. I became so interested in stocks that I convinced some of my friends to invest as well. In my junior year, I won second prize at the science fair for a display explaining how the stock market works. I really enjoyed my foray into finances.

However, in October of my junior year, I began to wonder whether I was becoming too focused on the stock market. Maybe it would affect my ministry when I became a priest. These questions lurked in my mind until Christmas, and during that time, I tried to become more detached from my investments. Looking back, this certainly helped me in my discernment process because three days after Christmas, an idea popped into my head: "I will not be a diocesan priest." This stunned me, but it seemed totally right. Three days later another idea popped in, equally surprising: "I will be a Jesuit." I had never met any Jesuits in my life. I had only heard about them here and there. However, this also seemed right.

Without informing my parents, I began talking to the Jesuit vocation director. This led to my reading about Jesuits. Finally, in February of my junior year, I announced at the dinner table: "I am going to enter the Jesuits." My dad's response was "What is he talking about now?" Once I explained it to him with my mom's help, he looked directly at me and told me that if I became a Jesuit priest, he would disinherit me. His firm tone indicated that he meant what he said. And right after my first Mass, he took me aside and said, "You know, this means you are out of my will." I smiled and nodded, thinking to myself that I would not be able to keep my inheritance in any case since we Jesuits take a vow of poverty. However, at least for that moment, even I was not so much of a wise guy to say this aloud to him. But I could freely say, "It doesn't matter to me because this is God's will. I can't let your concern of what you think my life should be like to determine what I'm going to do to serve God. I can't let that get in the way." I returned to the guests celebrating my first Mass and enjoyed the rest of the party.

Learning Detachment

Becoming detached from a fascination with the stock market was not the last step in complete open-mindedness to my vocation; other interests certainly presented themselves. At the beginning of our senior year at Quigley North Preparatory Seminary, Cardinal John Cody changed a number of our seminary rules. For instance, we had previously used an old European system of attending school on Saturday and having Thursday as a day off. At first this seemed odd, but it later became a rhythm for study, with a midweek break featuring a Wednesday-night card game or basketball game with other seminarians. It also served, as it was intended, to isolate us from the dances and football games on Friday and Saturday nights. Cardinal Cody wanted the seminarians to attend school on Thursdays and have the same two-day weekend as everyone else. He also made another change, granting us permission to go to dances, parties, and even on dates with girls. Previously the seminary rules had forbidden these activities so strongly that even attending a party with girls or a dance was grounds for dismissal from the seminary. Now we could go to dances and out on dates, apparently to give us opportunities to learn how to relate to young ladies better, as well as to test our commitment to celibacy. Frankly, I came to love going to Friday-night dances and Saturday sock hops at my friends' high schools (since hosting a dance at our high school seminary was still inconceivable).

Dating in the summer after senior year and during my freshman year of college was also a lot of fun. In the year I attended Loyola University, before entering the Jesuit Order, I dated Eileen, a young woman in my Spanish class. Once, while watching the re-release of *Gone with the Wind*, I began to think that all of the weddings in the movie looked like a wonderful idea. I turned and looked at Eileen to ask if she would marry me. Before saying a word, however, I thought, "I have recently applied to the Society of Jesus. I better think about such a serious question before I ask it." In fact, I had applied to the Jesuits during my senior year at Quigley, but the order had postponed my entrance, asking me to attend a Jesuit university for a while to let me mature and to give the Jesuits an opportunity to get to know me better. During my freshman year at Loyola, I applied again. I was frustrated by the earlier delay as well as nervous about whether I would be able to continue studying because the tuition costs at Loyola were high (the stock investments helped but were not enough). I also felt an attraction to Eileen, who was as sweet a girl as I ever expected to meet.

I brought the issue to prayer, feeling frustrated and agitated. But my response to these feelings was rather foolish. I told our Lord that if I did not get accepted by the Jesuits, then I would forget the priesthood and pursue marriage. The mistake lay in telling our Lord how to communicate with me, challenging him to respond to my demand for clarity rather than listening to his call as he desired to offer it—gently, quietly, and in more subtle ways. Though I had seen a wonderful television play about Gideon, I had not understood his mistake of demanding two signs from God: covering a fleece with dew while keeping the ground dry, and then keeping the fleece dry while making the ground wet with dew (Judges 6:36-40). Some Christians call this manner of testing God "fleecing the Lord." In my case, the "fleecing" turned out well, since I received my acceptance by the Society of Jesus with incredible joy. This felt like a great release from the way I had tested God, as well as gratitude for being accepted into the Jesuits.

A more mature approach (something of which I was not yet capable at that stage of my life) would have been to examine the various kinds of feelings I was experiencing about marriage to Eileen. I needed to pay attention to the fact that I was having an emotional response to a beautifully filmed novel rather than a stirring from the deeper desires of my heart. The strength of the romance stifled the years of peace that had been associated with thoughts of a vocation to the priesthood. Furthermore, I made demands on God rather than paying attention to the preceding movements of his Holy Spirit over the years of my short life. A year later, during my novitiate, I learned that St. Ignatius Loyola had once "fleeced the Lord" during his journey from the castle of Loyola to the Shrine of the Blessed Virgin Mary at Montserrat. A Muslim on a horse had engaged him in a conversation, which concluded when the Muslim insulted Our Lady. Ignatius left the decision to kill the Muslim up to his mule: If the mule followed the fork in the road taken by the Muslim, Ignatius would kill him; if not, then Ignatius would continue to Montserrat. In later years, Ignatius was always glad that the mule had exhibited much more sense than he did, just as Balaam's ass was better able than Balaam to discern the presence of God's spirit on the road to Moab (Numbers 22:21-34).

A final note regarding Eileen: I had one last date with her on the day before I entered the novitiate. That farewell picnic was very pleasant. I have always had fond memories of good times with her, including pleasant conversations on walks along Lake Michigan and fun parties with our friends. I had not maintained contact with her over the past forty years, but I recently learned that she passed away of cancer in 2008, much loved by a good husband and well remembered by many people she had helped at her church. God rest her soul.

For the Greater Glory of God

Another aspect of the discernment of my vocation to the priesthood was raised by my father when I was twelve years old. Dad sensed that I was probably the only one of my siblings who would go to college, and in fact he was right. Already knowing that my discussion about the priesthood was serious, he asked, "Why don't you become a doctor? You don't have to be a priest to help

people." Immediately I knew he was right. However, I responded
by saying, "Yes, but Dad, if I were a doctor and I healed people,
eventually they would still die anyway. If I heard their confession
on their deathbed and they went to heaven, it would last forever. It's a better deal!" My Father was a used-car salesman, so I
appealed to his professional side in regard to the "good deal." I
have to admit to being something of a smart aleck in those years,
but this time I was absolutely serious. In fact, I think this was a
kind of inspiration given to me, rooted in the Catholic teaching I
received from the Franciscan sisters at St. Priscilla School, to help
me recognize the greater good as the goal of life. Whenever we
look at the choices we are discerning, part of the process requires
that we ask God our Lord about the greater good that he wants
us to pursue. How will our decision give greater glory to God?
Equal-minded openness to God's will and his lordship over all the
good of creation that he has made is indispensable to answering
the question about how to give greater glory to God.

An afterthought about that conversation with my father
occurred to me about two years after he died. While telling this
story of my conversation with my dad to Mother Angelica on her
program, I suddenly realized that in my dad's final illness, he had
asked me to hear his confession. He had not been to confession
in a number of years, and he had always told me that he would
never confess to me. However, the day before his very serious
aneurysm surgery, he asked me to hear his confession. Knowing
his previously stated wishes, I even asked him if he wanted me to
find another priest. He insisted, and I heard his confession thirty-
two years after his suggestion that I become a doctor instead of
a priest. Had I become a doctor, I would not have been able to

perform surgery on him because he was a family member; as a priest I could serve him for eternal life.

Trusting in God's Unique Mission for Us

When we choose to give greater glory to God and move toward being equal-minded about any vocation, mission, or task that God may give us, we would do well to remember two things: first, that we need to be united with both Christ and his Church in all that we do; and second, that God will fit the vocation or mission to each particular individual. An insight into this reality comes from our reflecting on Matthew 11:28-30:

> "Come to me all you who labor and are heavy-burdened and I will give you rest. Take my yoke upon you, and learn from me; for I am gentle and lowly in heart, and you will find rest for your souls. For my yoke is easy and my burden is light."

This passage has captured the hearts of weary people through the ages, but a little background on yokes may help us understand it in a new light. A yoke is a wooden bar, with another piece of wood that curves under the ox's neck and comes up through the bar, with a pin or straps to hold the neck piece in place. The yoke is connected to a plow, wagon, or other instrument that is to be pulled by a pair of oxen, usually side by side. Yokes are not carved so that one size fits all oxen; they need to be handcrafted by a carpenter so that the bar and lower piece fit the particular ox pulling it. Carpenters design the yokes to fit each particular ox to prevent chafing on its chest and shoulder. (St. Justin Martyr, during a visit to his homeland in Samaria, was shown a yoke that was said to have been crafted by Jesus, and he noted how very well made it was. This indicates that Jesus, an expert carpenter, understood what he was saying about yokes.)

The Need to Be Yoked to Christ and His Church

Yokemaking can give us insight into God's call for us: Christ will give us a yoke that is precisely made for each one of us. No "one-size-fits-all" vocation is handed out as if it were being mass-produced. Even when a group of people share a certain religious vocation—for instance, the seven hundred boys in my freshman class at high school seminary, or the ten men in my novitiate class—each person lives out the life Christ gives to each one, despite so much of the exterior uniformity in certain aspects of the training or clothing style.

This same principle applies to the vocation of marriage: Each marriage is a yoke unique to each couple and to each person within the family. Notice the wide variety of ways in which the tasks of marriage—raising children, communicating within the family, handling finances, resolving disagreements—are handled by each couple. Not every husband is good at balancing the bank statement, and neither is every wife the better cook. The gifts and talents of each member of the pair will be recognized and used in distinctive ways, just as each yoke is fitted for each particular ox. Each one of us would do well to prayerfully reflect on the ways in which we can better see that Christ has customized our "yokes" and placed them on our shoulders, not on someone else's.

This image of the yoke can help us further understand that the acceptance of the vocation the Lord gives each of us will necessarily entail the exclusion of many good components of other vocations. My acceptance of the priesthood excludes the many goods of marriage—the love and companionship of a wife, the joy of children, as well as the responsibilities and opportunities for personal growth and holiness that these entail. The person who gets married will not have the public leadership of celebrating Mass or other sacraments. However, by choosing the vocation Christ Jesus has given me, and by peacefully resigning myself to

The process of accepting God's vocation and mission entails an ongoing discernment

"missing out" on the other vocations, I am placing a profound level of trust in God that this vocation he has chosen for me is the one that fits me best. By accepting God's call, by recognizing that this fits my personality best as God sees my heart and soul, and by trusting that his call will best serve the rest of the Church and humanity, I can give greater glory to God in all that I do.

The emphasis I have just given to the uniquely designed quality of the vocational and apostolic yokes Christ places upon our shoulders can be misinterpreted and distorted by popular modern thought. Many contemporaries fear that they may lose their individuality in a society of mass production and consumption. A modern proclamation of individualistic identity and style was sung in songs announcing "I gotta be me!" or "I did it my way," with variations of that theme appearing in all genres. This idea permeates the popular mentality. Modern people may fear not being distinctive, but in order to be unique, they often take on worldly forms of "sameness." For example, they may tattoo their skin in order to differentiate themselves from others, but they choose those tattoo patterns from a catalog. The latest fashion styles are also evidence of this phenomenon.

The process of accepting God's vocation and mission entails an ongoing discernment in regard to the ways Christ wants us to go and how he wants us to accomplish the tasks he sets before us. Here it is useful to return to the first two chapters. While our Lord wants to save all men and women and have them know the truth (1 Timothy 2:4), this mission may not be accomplished by threatening to kill anyone who does not comply, as was the case with the Teutonic knights in Lithuania and a few other groups of missionaries in Church history. Neither can we falsify the gospel of Christ by adding untruths or by neglecting some truths, since the objective norm of God's revelation requires Christians to never bear false witness. God does not want us to accomplish his mission "our way" but in accordance with his just, charitable, virtuous, and holy ways.

Avoiding a "Lone Ranger" Mentality

Another way in which individualism can distort the unique quality of one's vocation and mission is through trying to accomplish our work with a "lone ranger" mentality—trying to save the world without help from others. Some people fear the imposition of directions, orders, or rules from other people, especially from distant Church officials. Others wonder, "How can I work with people in the Church who do not appreciate my sacrifices or who do not understand my unique genius?" They may fear being directed away from their vision of the mission into a completely different and perhaps even meaningless task. Hence, they want to go it alone without communal and authoritarian complications.

However, our distinctive qualities can exist only when we are united to Jesus Christ and to his Church. First, the yoke Christ places upon our shoulders includes his companionship as a yoke

> The yoke Christ places upon our shoulders includes his companionship as a yoke mate.

mate. If I separate myself from our Lord, I have thereby broken the yoke and am pulling in a direction contrary to his. The next chapter will discuss more about the ways we stay connected to Christ through prayer. However, at this point it is important to understand the necessity of remaining yoked to Jesus Christ if indeed we are to take on ourselves his "easy" yoke.

Even if most Christians agree to being yoked to Christ, they still might object to working with those in the Church. Therefore, the second point, and often the more difficult one, is that we belong to a long chain of oxen yoked together: the Church. Of course, a far more apt image of the Church is the one given by St. Paul when he identifies the Church as the "body of Christ" (1 Corinthians 12–14; Ephesians 4). It is this image of the Church as a body that helps us better understand the necessity of being united with the Church if we are to remain distinctive individually. Biologically each human body is a unified whole with a wide diversity of organs within that whole body. It is precisely because of the unity of the human body that the diverse array of individual organs can work together. Christians who isolate themselves and who are not united with Jesus Christ and one another ironically risk losing their identity and becoming just like everyone else. Perhaps they fall into sin or strive only for material success. On the other hand, the more united we are to Christ and his Church, the more distinctive we become—because Christ has in mind exactly the mission or vocation he wants for us. A look at the diversity of saints of the Church through the ages vividly demonstrates this truth. What follows is a description of three modern-day heroes of our faith who were led by God to fulfill a mission that was uniquely theirs.

The Unique Missions of Three Great Modern-Day Saints

I have been privileged to know Mother Angelica for twenty-five years. She is a classic example of a person who has shone out into the world because her number-one love is Jesus Christ and his Church. When she became disabled during an accident in the convent, she promised Jesus that she would open a convent in the southern states (which were mission territory for Catholics) if she were able to walk again. When this prayer was answered, she sold fishing lures in order to buy the land for a convent in Irondale, Alabama. She later began writing pamphlets to promote the spiritual life in a way that any person could understand. She gave Bible studies and then lectures, and even made some television programs.

Mother Angelica was angered when she learned about the airing of a controversial and irreverent television program about

Jesus. In prayer she felt called to start a television network, even though the convent she had started had only two hundred dollars in the bank. Slowly she gathered the loans, equipment, personnel, and other resources necessary to launch the Eternal Word Television Network (EWTN). This network would eventually broadcast twenty-four-hour television and radio programming in Spanish and English formats, with German and French programs in Europe. A formerly disabled nun with two hundred dollars founded a global network that now reaches one hundred and eighty million homes by television and still more by radio in the vast majority of the world's countries.

Blessed Mother Teresa of Calcutta generously went to India as a missionary to teach young girls. However, after experiencing a certain desolation regarding her mission as a teacher, she heard a call from God to serve the poorest of the poor in Calcutta. The community she founded, the Missionaries of Charity, has spread around the world, helping the poor and destitute on every continent and treating people with diseases such as leprosy and AIDS. She has become the icon of goodness and generosity, not only for Catholics, but also for Protestants, Jews, and even Muslims, Hindus, and atheists. She has already been beatified, and the faithful expect her to be canonized; people already pray for her intercession, and her life will be celebrated for years to come. In contrast, in future ages today's rich and famous will be long forgotten.

Another modern saint-to-be is Pope John Paul II, a survivor of World War II who lost his mother as a child, his only brother as an adolescent, and his father as a young adult. He was forced to end his studies because the Nazis required that he work. After his father died, he discerned a call to the priesthood. With no immediate family and possessing only the brains that God had given him and a heart transformed by grace, he knocked on the door of the archbishop's home in Krakow and sought acceptance in the clandestine seminary located in the archbishop's home. Eventually he became archbishop of Krakow, and in 1978 he was elected pope. His papacy inspired not only Catholics but people throughout the world, and his writings will continue to influence the Church well into the next millennium. Already people call him "John Paul the Great," a title that currently belongs to only two other popes, Leo I and Gregory I.

These three modern saints simply pursued union with Christ and his Church. All were deeply committed to obeying the proper authorities within the Church as they sought to bring the good news of Jesus in word and deed to as many people as they could. None of them were likely candidates for world renown, but all three are household names who will be remembered more than the prime ministers, corporate presidents, athletes, and actors of the same period. Such saints accept from Christ the yoke that fits them uniquely. They do not try to imitate other famous people, nor do they seek to promote their careers. They discern God's will and listen to him as best they can.

Questions for Reflection and Discussion

1. Why might we be afraid to admit wrongdoing? How can we counter these fears so that we can experience the peace that comes with repentance and reconciliation?

2. When have you made a decision after praying through it first? Did these prayers consist more of a one-way or two-way form of communication? Do you believe that your prayers helped you to discover God's will in the matter?

3. How does knowing God's love for us personally help us to become more "equal-minded"?

4. When has an attachment prevented you from hearing God and doing his will? Were you able to become more detached when you recognized it as an obstacle? Are there any attachments in your life right now that you should you let go of?

5. Do you believe that God has a unique mission for you, one that is tailor made just for you in this time in history? How can this truth help you when you are struggling or in doubt of that mission?

CHAPTER 5

COMMUNICATING
WITH GOD

The Many Ways to Pray

In the last chapter, we used the image of being yoked to Christ to highlight the uniqueness of each person's vocation from God. Another way to look at Christ's yoke is to remember that yokes are designed for two oxen, an image that can apply to Jesus and the person who accepts the call to take on his easy yoke—made easy because Jesus is the other ox pulling our burden with us. As is generally true of oxen, one is stronger than the other, and the stronger ox pulls the greater weight with the yoke. In the case of the vocational yoke Christ places upon us, he is the stronger ox, doing the heavy pulling through our spiritual life and vocational struggles, constantly at our side. However, we weaker oxen who are yoked to Christ need to maintain good communication with him, both to pay attention to his ongoing leadership and to know the infinite love he has for us.

The communication we humans have with God is known as prayer. Each of the ways we communicate with others has a purpose, and each is quite good and useful within its proper realm. This same principle applies to prayer. What is important is that we realize that just as we have the freedom to communicate in many ways to our loved ones, so do we have the freedom to communicate with God in prayer, in many ways and on many levels of depth.

Some people may not even start to pray because they know they do not pray as deeply as the great mystics of times past. Some may be tempted to think that if they use the traditional prayers that they memorized as children, they will be praying superficially. Others may be frustrated because the only time they have to pray is when they pray with their children. If one remains only on a superficial level with God in prayer, dissatisfaction can be expected. But such dissatisfaction does not mean you should pray differently or abandon prayer altogether. It is simply a call to deepen your prayer.

High points of prayer cannot be sustained through every moment of every day. Until the time that we attain the direct vision of God in heaven, there is a role for short prayers and

> High points of prayer cannot be sustained through every moment of every day.

memorized prayers as well as profound contemplation. This variety of methods, styles, and depths of prayer helps us maintain an awareness of the presence of God. So let's look at the different types of communication we use in everyday life, and then apply these examples to prayer.

How We Communicate with Others

In daily life people pass each other, say hello, and ask, "How are you doing?" Most of the time we expect the other person to answer, "Fine, how are you?" so that we can continue on with our daily routine. In fact, at times we may dread when people try to answer that question in more detail. But is that type of conversation worthless because it remains at the expected level of superficiality? No, not at all. Though it skims the surface, it serves to keep the various people aware of each other's presence in a friendly way, and it encourages a pleasant atmosphere in which to work and live. And sometimes these greetings do develop into deeper sharing and conversation.

In family life many levels of communication exist. There may be quiet times, perhaps in the late evenings, when there is a sense of trust, acceptance, and comfort that pervades the home. Although it may be a practice that is fading in the modern culture, the family dinner hour remains an extremely important time for family talk and business to take place. Table conversation reveals what is going on in the life of each member of the family. Family dinners also provide opportunities for parents to teach children their faith as well as their manners, and to discuss current events and other important issues.

We also have times in which very important personal conversations occur between two or more individuals. In particular, husbands and wives need times in which to talk, apart from children interrupting or demanding their attention. Parents need to share with each other what is going on inside of them, how they feel, what is really moving them, what really bothers them, and how much they love each other. When intimacy is a normal part of the couple's relationship, the family has a center from which the members can resolve tensions and move forward.

Other opportunities for communication and conversation occur during family vacations, camping trips, or excursions of parents with individual children. Fishing and hunting trips might not include a lot of talking, especially if Dad and the boys are involved, but the time spent together is very important and may create a bond that affects the relationships for years. In addition, important communication occurs when children are being corrected and disciplined for misbehavior. My dad certainly said many times, "Someday you'll thank me for this." Never did I thank him on that day, but many the day has come when I have thanked him—obviously indicative of the long-term impact of a short-term communication.

Communicating with God at Mass

These various levels and types of communication that occur in normal relationships and in family life are analogous to our prayer relationship with God. Communal prayer, especially at Mass, is as important to the Church as shared meals are to the family. The Eucharist is the "source and the summit of our Christian life," as Vatican II teaches (*Lumen gentium,* 11) and as Pope John Paul II has reiterated in his letters and encyclicals. In fact, the idea of the Eucharist as the "source and summit" goes back to St. Thomas Aquinas (*Summa Theologiae*, III, q. 73, a. 3c). What does this mean? The Eucharist is the source of our spiritual life because it is Jesus Christ whom we receive—body, blood, soul, and divinity— and only he can be the source of strength to live out our Christian life. The Eucharist is the high point, or summit, of the spiritual life because it is our deepest union with Christ.

Just as a family needs to eat its meals together in order to get along and be nourished, so also do we need the Eucharist in order to be nourished with Christ's Body and Blood and to attain eternal life (John 6:53-54). The Mass is also a celebration with the extended family of the Church. Some celebrations of the Mass are extra special, such as the important feasts of Christmas and Easter, and may feature special music, incense, and altar flowers. These very important communal celebrations are analogous to those large family celebrations and reunions that bring many relatives together for a special occasion. Just as family reunions are never as intimate as small family dinners, neither are the large sacramental celebrations as intimate as the daily parish Mass. Yet these different kinds of Eucharistic celebrations complement one another, just as an intimate candlelight dinner complements the wedding feast.

One-on-One Time with God

However, in addition to large communal celebrations, we need to have those quiet times when we commune with God in our hearts. Just as a husband and wife need to communicate on an intimate level, sharing their hearts with each other, so, too, do we need that intimate level of sharing with God. Without that private prayer time, how will we ever experience the deep peace of God that surpasses all understanding? (Philippians 4:7).

At times the parish church can be as busy and even as hectic as a large family. During Mass children cry and people come and go, walking fidgety babies or escorting panicked children to the restroom. It is easy to be distracted by these things, but a more personal prayer relationship with Christ that takes place outside of Mass makes it possible to be more centered and focused on Christ during the celebration of the Eucharist. Our private prayer time and personal union with Christ nourish whatever we do in the public sphere of the church. Every Christian, not just those who are in the religious life, needs to have quiet time with Christ that nourishes the public life, whether in the liturgy or outside it.

A few points about the quality of intimacy in prayer are in order here. The first point is that traditional prayers need not be treated as something inferior to the spontaneous prayers that come from a person's heart. Spontaneous prayer, sincerely expressed, may be a very important way to speak to the Lord. However, the prayers that we have received from the Church are important ways of teaching us how to pray in theologically correct ways and may even be superior if our spontaneous prayers express untrue notions of God or our relationship to him. The traditional prayers often come from Sacred Scripture. For example, the Our Father was taught to us by Jesus; the Hail Mary is a combination of the words of the angel Gabriel (Luke 1:28) and St. Elizabeth (1:42) when they addressed the Blessed Virgin.

A traditional prayer memorized by most Catholics early in life is the Act of Contrition. Too often we say it quickly with nervous relief after having confessed our sins and having been given a penance. However, it is filled with great depth and warrants additional reflection:

- *O my God.* We are speaking directly to our Lord, and this is enough to awaken reflection on the words.
- *I am heartily sorry for having offended you.* This sentence indicates that our sorrow flows from the depths of our heart and therefore is a profound expression of our deepest selves.

- *I detest all my sins because I dread the loss of heaven and the pains of hell.* Sin is not merely some mildly excusable faux pas but a detestable act with grave consequences. As we discussed in chapter one, the issue of avoiding hell and getting to heaven is one of the most important in all of life.

- *But most of all because they offend you, who are all good and deserving of all my love.* This profession of faith shows that sin goes far beyond a fear of punishment or loss of reward but to the very love that is above all loves. Underlying this sentence is the commandment of God to love him with our whole heart, mind, and soul (Deuteronomy 6:5; Matthew 22:37).

- *I firmly resolve, with the help of your grace, to sin no more and to avoid the near occasion of sin.* This resolution recognizes that not only must we make a firm decision to avoid committing the sin again but that we also need the help of God's grace to maintain that resolve. We cannot remain faithful to God unless his grace makes it possible, and yet he expects us to make that act of the will so that we will be open to his grace. Not only do we want to avoid the actual sin, but we plan to stay away from the circumstances that will open the possibility of committing that sin or making it more likely.

This short, very traditional liturgical prayer may be said many hundreds of times, but taking the time to meditate upon it more thoroughly will make each repetition more meaningful. One penitent told me that he says the prayer as if his life depends on it—and it does. Taking the time to meditate on the other traditional prayers of the Church will also help them to come alive for us.

The official prayer book of the Church since its earliest days has been the psalms. The psalms are organized in the Liturgy of the Hours, also known as the Divine Office, along with various canticles and hymns from both the Old and New Testaments as well as Scripture readings and other prayers. The Liturgy of the Hours divides the day into times of prayer and teaches its users to sanctify each portion of the day. We need these traditional formula prayers to teach us how to pray and to guide our words when we pray spontaneously.

The second point about the quality of intimacy in prayer is that we should avoid talking so much to God in our prayer that we do not give him a chance to speak back to us. Sometimes we can say so many prayers, whether traditional or spontaneous, that we give

> We should avoid talking so much to God in our prayer that we do not give him a chance to speak back to us.

our Lord no opportunity to address our hearts. Listening to God means allowing an attentive silence that makes it possible to hear him speak to us in the intimacy of our hearts. At times we may sense words being addressed to us interiorly; at other times we may simply experience a calming peace and love. At times there may be a hollow emptiness. Sometimes we may not like hearing what the Lord has to say because it corrects or challenges our behavior and expectations. Whatever we hear must be discerned, as was described in the previous chapter. But at the least, we should give God a chance to speak to us. In the next chapter, we will describe some prayer techniques that can help this listening process.

Short Aspirations and Litanies

It's important to remember that not every moment of private personal prayer will be filled with ecstasy or profound insight. Just as our daily life in the family includes the common pleasantries, so also does a normal prayer life include less intense types of prayer.

Sometimes these are very short one-liners, such as "Jesus, have mercy on me." Such prayers are called aspirations. They may be as simple as a mention of "Jesus, Mary, and Joseph." Examples of such short aspirations can also be found in many prayer books, especially from times past.

Another way of praying short aspirations is by the use of litanies. A litany is usually a series of short aspirations directed to the Lord God, to the Blessed Mother, or to one of the saints. The aspirations are linked together according to some theme, based on Sacred Scripture or the life of a particular saint. In litanies addressed to God, each aspiration usually describes one of our Lord's qualities and then evokes the response "Lord, have mercy" or "Hear us" or "Graciously hear us." When the litany is addressed to the Blessed Virgin Mary, a particular saint, or a group of saints, the response is "Pray for us." That's because Catholics do not expect the saints to do what only God can do, such as answer our prayers or bestow mercy upon us; the saints are fellow human beings who pray for us and intercede because they are already in heaven and therefore are closer to God.

Therefore, one of the ways of seeking the intercession of the saints is through praying the litanies. Like many quick greetings and pleasantries, it is possible to simply speak the words of the aspirations. However, just as those everyday pleasantries like "How are you?" can turn into a serious conversation when the person asking that question recognizes a look of deep sadness or joyful excitement in the other, so also can the aspirations of the litanies turn into a more profound type of prayer. Notice that everyday pleasantries can turn into a deeper conversation when at least one or both of the people have an authentic underlying love for one another. Similarly, people who authentically love God and his saints will be more prone to let an aspiration change into something deeper and more meditative.

For example, the Litany of Loretto expresses the titles of the Virgin Mary quite poetically. When we pray the title "Ark of the Covenant," we can ask ourselves, "How is Mary the ark of the covenant?" Then as we consider that she bore the infant Jesus in her womb, we can understand that Jesus personifies the new covenant, and in a certain way, Mary is the ark who bore him. Then our minds may think of the overshadowing of God's presence on the ark in the Old Testament and connect it with the overshadowing of the Holy Spirit by which Jesus was conceived in Mary's womb. We may further consider the revelation of the ark of the covenant in Revelation 11:19, the very last mention of the ark in the whole Bible, and then continue reading the very next verses (Revelation 12:1ff), which portray a vision of Mary bearing her son, Jesus, and giving birth to him. So this one aspiration opens up a whole series of meditations for the person who is open to deeper consideration of the image. The rest of the aspirations—such as "Tower of David," "Gate of Heaven," "Seat of Wisdom," the "Mystic Rose," and so on—can open up deep reflection and a rich search into Sacred Scripture as well. A charming example of such reflection appears in G. K. Chesterton's poem, "A Little Litany," in which Chesterton pictures the baby Jesus crawling up into the lap of Mary and looking into her eyes:

> When God turned back eternity and was young,
> Ancient of Days, grown little for your mirth
> (As under the low arch the land is bright)
> Peered through you, gate of heaven—and saw the earth.
>
> Or shutting out his shining skies awhile
> Built you about him for a house of gold
> To see in pictured walls his storied world
> Return upon him as a tale is told.
>
> Or found his mirror there; the only glass
> That would not break with that unbearable light
> Till in a corner of that high dark house
> God looked on God, as ghosts meet in the night.
>
> Star of his morning; that unfallen star
> In the strange starry overturn of space
> When earth and sky changed places for an hour
> And heaven looked upwards in a human face.
>
> Or young on your strong knees and lifted up
> Wisdom cried out, whose voice is in the street,
> And more than twilight of twiformed cherubim
> Made of his throne indeed a mercy seat.

Or risen from play at your pale raiment's hem
God, grown adventurous from all time's repose,
Of your tall body climbed the ivory tower
And kissed upon your mouth the mystic rose.

Similar meditation can be applied to the litanies of the Sacred Heart of Jesus, the Infant Jesus, the Most Holy Name of Jesus, and the Holy Spirit. In praying the various litanies of the saints, we can consider the virtues of the saints and seek to imitate their holiness. Both the quick prayer of the litany and the reflection on each petition can be very useful, whether in establishing a tone of prayer throughout the day or in going deeper with a more profound meditation.

Prayers of Praise

Another type of quick prayer was inspired by a wonderful little book called *Prison to Praise* by Merlin Carothers. Carothers served time in a military prison and then saw combat in World War II. After his conversion, he was serving as a pastor when God told him to stop complaining about his difficulties and start praising God precisely for those problems. He thought this was odd, but he listened to God and began to praise him in everything. This filled him with joy, and he learned to trust that God was working even in difficult situations and that it was ultimately for his benefit.

An image of a parked car has helped me understand this idea of praising God for our problems. When a car is parked, one can turn the steering wheel, but it takes a bit of effort. In contrast, when a car is in motion, the wheel turns with a flick of the wrist. Similarly, when we are upset, anxious, and complaining about our problems, we are like a parked car. Our Lord can redirect us, but we resist his efforts. However, when we begin praising the Lord for our difficulties, then we are like that car in motion. Praising God for our problems and not despite them does not mean that we necessarily feel elated, giddy, or happy about those problems. We may still feel the same sadness and grief for the difficulty. However, despite our feeling, we make an act of the will to praise God anyway. That act of the will is what our Lord can more easily redirect. Eventually both peace and joy will return, but they will come not just because we may have gotten what we wanted but because we see God active and present in our lives.

A short aspiration during stress and difficulties can be very simple. "Praise you, Lord, that I hit my thumb with the hammer." "Praise you, Lord, for the sickness I am enduring." "Praise you,

> A short aspiration during stress and difficulties can be very simple.

Lord, because I do not have the money I need to take care of my family." And this can be repeated each time one considers the problem. At times I even thank God that I feel anxious. That is far better than getting upset with myself for not having trusted our Lord more fully. With this attitude of praise operative in my mind, I can then say with Paul, "All things work out to the good for those who love God" (Romans 8:28). My problems and my failures can even work to the good, even though I may not see how they all work out and I may not appreciate the slowness of

God's timing. However, I trust that with this short aspiration of praise, he will bring great good out of a situation from which I can see no escape.

The Rosary

The beauty of the Rosary is that it can be prayed on so many levels, in so many places, individually or communally. If we continue with our analogies of the ways we communicate with others, we could say that the Rosary is the prayer that spans a wide variety of human interactions. Because the prayers of the Rosary are memorized, we can pray it while doing other tasks, as if we were washing the dishes but at the same time enjoying the company of our family. We can pray it with others, analogous to a family get-together. Or we can spend intimate moments with Jesus as we contemplate the mysteries of his life and death.

Most Catholics are very familiar with the Rosary, but many are surprised when they discover the level of depth that is possible while "telling the beads." An essential component of the Rosary is the association of one of the mysteries of Christ's life with each decade. The importance of these mysteries was well expressed by Pope Paul VI, who called them the "soul" of the Rosary (*Marialis cultus*, 47) because it is precisely in these meditations that we come to know the various aspects of Jesus Christ's work to save the world from sin and separation from God. The first set of five mysteries are called "Joyful" and meditate on Jesus' birth, infancy, and childhood, especially as recorded in St. Luke's Gospel. The Luminous Mysteries consider key events from Christ's public ministry. The Sorrowful Mysteries consider his suffering and death, and the Glorious Mysteries consider his resurrection and its aftermath.

There are a number of reasons to meditate on these mysteries while praying the ten Hail Marys of each decade. First, we learn to approach each mystery from the perspective of the Blessed Virgin Mary. Recall that Our Lady was present at many of these events, not only in the events surrounding Jesus' birth, but also at the wedding feast of Cana and while Jesus carried his cross and was crucified. She was with the apostles in the upper room at Pentecost, so we can also safely assume that she saw the risen Lord Jesus and perhaps his ascension. Of course, she experienced her own assumption and crowning in heaven. By repeating the Hail Mary, we address her with those greetings of St. Gabriel and St. Elizabeth, and then we ask for her prayers as we consider the mysteries. In this process, it is as if we were trying to look at

> The Virgin Mary can always lead us to a deeper love and a more uplifting perspective of faith in Christ.

each mystery of salvation from her maternal perspective, seeking to love Jesus Christ, the center of each mystery, as she does. I assume that the Virgin Mary had a more personal and a more highly motivated love of Jesus than we sinners do. As much as we may love Christ, the Virgin Mary can always lead us to a deeper love and a more uplifting perspective of faith in him.

Another reason to keep returning to these mysteries is to integrate the cycle of all twenty mysteries into the rhythm of our lives. At times the temptation may be to focus on the mysteries we like—perhaps the warmth of the nativity or the glory of the resurrection or the power of Pentecost. While it is permissible to feel drawn to emphasize a certain aspect of the mystery of salvation, as do many of the religious orders—the Passionists or the Resurrectionists, for example—the Christian faith encompasses all aspects of salvation. Praying through the cycle of the twenty mysteries will remind us to balance our meditation on all the key mysteries of salvation.

Some people pray the Rosary while driving or walking; because the prayers are memorized, this is easy to do. And given the temptation we all face to express anger at other drivers, we may find that praying a Rosary while we drive is a constructive thing to do! It's also a good way to keep a prayerful attitude while performing a task that might lend itself to distraction. Two friends can take a walk and pray the Rosary aloud, or a whole parish can pray the Rosary together, as we do at St. Elias Maronite Parish every Sunday before the 10:30 a.m. *Qurbono* (Aramaic for "Mass").

Many people pray the Rosary in church or in a private room of the house that is free of distractions. The quiet and the greater attention that are possible in such an environment can enable us to take more time to concentrate on the individual mysteries of the Rosary. A variety of aids to meditating on the mysteries are available, including books or pamphlets called "Scriptural Rosaries," which provide one verse of Scripture for each Hail Mary in every decade, or those with short reflections on each mystery. A person might do well to look up the mysteries in the Bible and read a small part of that passage, either at the beginning of each decade or in small sections between each Hail Mary. Other people simply focus on their own imaginative sense of each mystery, while still others concentrate on the words of the Hail Mary, the Our Father, or the Glory Be. Everyone is free to approach the Rosary according to one's own preference. However, the more open in heart and mind we are to the prayers and the mysteries, the greater will be the depth of prayer we experience.

Praying with Children

For families, the Rosary is an ideal way to pray together. Fr. Patrick Peyton, the famous "Rosary Priest," coined the phrase "The family that prays together stays together." He not only organized Rosary rallies around the world, but he actively promoted praying the Rosary in families.

Parents and children can pray the Rosary together quite easily, even when the children are very young. In their early years, it may suffice to pray only one decade together since the attention span of children is so short. However, children may be better able to pay attention if they can lead the Rosary. This helps them to recognize that they have an important role in the prayer. I have enjoyed many evenings with families who do just that. Of course, a few words may be omitted by a two- or three-year-old, and the little voice may begin to sound sleepy, but there is no doubt that our Lord and his mother delight in these prayers. Another good practice is to ask each child to say the intention they are praying for. When children are focused on a particular intention, they take the matter quite seriously.

In general, praying with our children is one of the joys of being around them. One of the highly treasured moments of most parents is their invitation to children to start praying aloud once they learn to speak. Parents can repeat prayers enough times until the children memorize them. As most parents realize, children often play the same movie or sing the same song over and over again; it's usually the parents, not the children, who tire of the repetition. When teaching children to pray, parents can help children memorize the traditional prayers as well as encourage them to

> Praying with our children is one of the joys of being around them.

speak to God in their own words. Parents lead the children by letting prayer permeate life—grace before meals, morning and evening prayers, and at other times of the day, as when news of an illness or a problem arises.

These many opportunities to pray with our children and to pray as a family will be formative for everyone. However, there still remains the need for more intimate and personal prayer than is possible in these shared moments with the family. Such intimacy with God requires quiet time, a scarce commodity during some seasons of life. Parents with little children at home, especially babies, might get a snippet of quiet time here and there. But when a baby starts to cry, a parent cannot say to them, "Honey, stop crying; I'm talking to God here!" In fact, performing one's duty to meet the needs of a crying baby or a hungry child is a wonderful way to listen to our Lord, who said in regard to the hungry, thirsty, naked, and sick, "Whatever you do to the least of my brothers, you do to me" (Matthew 25:40). Nevertheless, just as husbands and wives find time for personal moments and intimacies in between changing diapers and feeding children, so also can the believer find those small moments that refresh the soul. The prayer might be more vocal, such as the aspirations or the Rosary; it might be the recitation of short devotions from a favorite prayer book or the Bible. But these are still nourishing to the tired parent.

As children grow up and move out, parents may be able to find more time for private prayer, a retreat, or some other way to be alone with Jesus. Once the kids are out of the house and there is quiet, a person has to decide whether to fill the silence with more activities or make more time to be alone with God. Only the individual can make the choice to put God on the high-priority list.

We began this chapter by noting that we are yoked to Christ. We need prayer so that we can allow him to lead us and so that we can know his love. In the next chapter, we'll talk more about prayer, specifically about praying with the Scriptures, through which we can allow God to speak to us.

Questions for Reflection and Discussion

1. How does it help to compare the way we pray with the way we communicate with our family and friends? Why should we take advantage of the many different ways to communicate with God?

2. Which traditional prayer most speaks to your heart? Why? Think about someone with whom you can share this prayer and ask God to show you the right time and way to do so.

3. Do you offer up short prayers to God throughout your day? How do these help you? What other times in your schedule would such prayers help you to maintain an awareness and connection with the Lord?

4. Have you ever praised God for some problem or difficulty you were experiencing? How might God use such a prayer to change your heart?

5. Is the Rosary part of your prayer life? Do you believe that praying just one decade of the Rosary could be powerful form of prayer? How can you make the Rosary a more meaningful prayer in your life?

CHAPTER 6

HEARING GOD IN
HIS WORD

The "Five Ps" of Praying with Scripture

Catholics hear the Scriptures at every Mass, and the prayers of the liturgy are filled with Scripture quotations and allusions to Scripture. But we can also use the Scriptures in our quiet times to prayerfully listen to God speaking to our hearts. Sacred Scripture has always been a rich source of private prayer and meditation for Christians. In this chapter, I want to show you how you can pray with Scripture to listen to God. Before we begin, however, let's review the Church's teachings on Scripture.

The Church has always taught that Sacred Scripture is the word of God and that every word in it is inspired by God. At the same time, the Church understands that the Holy Spirit spoke through many different human authors of the Bible. Here is how the Second Vatican Council fathers explained it:

The books of both the Old and New Testaments in their entirety, with all their parts, are sacred and canonical because written under the inspiration of the Holy Spirit, they have God as their author and have been handed on as such to the Church herself. In composing the sacred books, God chose men and while employed by him they made use of their powers and abilities, so that with him acting in them and through them, they, as true authors, consigned to writing everything and only those things which he wanted. (*Dei verbum*, 11)

This means that God did not dictate his words to these authors; they truly spoke through their own personalities. This is evident when one examines the many different literary styles in the Bible. For example, the Hebrew of Hosea is in a northern dialect, while the Hebrew of Isaiah is in the southern dialect (he was from Jerusalem). The New Testament writers also demonstrate significant differences in style that reflect their personalities and backgrounds.

One image for understanding this situation is to see the Holy Spirit as the photographer, and the evangelists and other inspired writers of the Old and New Testaments as different kinds of cameras. Cameras are available in many styles, from little disposable cameras to expensive 35 mm cameras with many lenses. Each type of camera reflects the truth of the scene, but its limits and strengths give a different type of photograph of that scene. So also with the divinely inspired writers of Scripture: Each of them tells the truth about what God shows them, but we would do well to understand how they look at things, their perspectives, and their limits. For instance, St. Mark's Greek is more limited than St. Luke's, but that does not deny that St. Mark tells us the truth about Christ. Catholics fully proclaim that the Holy Spirit guided these sacred authors to see the truths necessary to live according to God's plan and to receive the redemption he prepared in Israel and won for us through Jesus Christ and his Church.

The task of Scripture scholars is to analyze the vocabulary, the organizational style, and the historical background of each book, as well as the theological perspective that emerges from the sacred writer, so as to better understand Scripture. This type of study better prepares us to listen to the message God is offering through the text—though the lack of in-depth Scripture study is no reason to avoid praying with Scripture. Over the centuries millions have prayed with Scripture without having a great deal of technical knowledge about the Bible's history and languages.

Once we accept in faith that God is truly the author of Scripture, we can approach the texts with an extremely important perspective: Let God, who inspired the words and authors

> Let God, who inspired the words and authors of the Sacred Scriptures, speak to us through them.

of the Sacred Scriptures, speak to us through them. While we can use the Scriptures to demonstrate the biblical basis for our faith—an important task—this is different than listening to God speak to us in the depths of our soul through the Scriptures. We need to learn how to allow the Scriptures to come into our lives and, like a two-edged sword, pierce our soul and spirit to their very depths. Through Scripture, God can form us and bring our minds and our hearts more fully into conformity with his. Listening to God through Scripture helps us learn to think with the mind of God and to love with the heart of God.

Prayer Is a Gift of God's Grace

How do we approach Scripture in order to prayerfully listen to God speaking to our hearts? The first step will be to ask the Holy Spirit who inspired the words of Scripture to stir within our hearts and inspire us both to understand the Scripture and hear him speak through them. Underlying this request for the Holy Spirit's help is the belief that prayer is a gift of God's grace. Prayer is not a technique that is under our personal control; it is not a method by which we can guarantee or attain a certain state of consciousness. Rather, prayer is a gift of a personal relationship with God, who personally reaches into the depths of our hearts and minds and lovingly addresses our needs, questions, and desires. God our Lord is not under our control; he initiates the relationship and graciously guides it in such a way as to make us

> Prayer is a gift of a personal relationship with God.

far better and more loving than we would ever know how to be on our own. Our role in the relationship is to seek him and ask for his help with a respect for his divine dignity, such as I might show to my fellow human beings.

This is not unlike a baby learning how to speak. Babies obviously feel quite pleased with themselves that they can speak and that the parents can understand. However, no one should forget that long before the child uttered a sound, the parents were lovingly waiting for that child to be born and then spent much time and energy nourishing and caring for the baby. All the while the parents speak to the infant, repeating words, making eye contact, smiling, and comforting. Only a year or so after birth does the child draw on this preparation and speak his or her first word. The learning continues as the child grows. This is possible only because the relationships that motivated speech were initiated before the child could speak. Similarly, God loves and cares for us long before we begin to pray. He remains with us as we learn how to speak to him—a lifelong process of improving our communication skills. Still, the grace of prayer is always the first step; our efforts are a response to God's fatherly initiative to love and nourish us.

Though our prayer depends on the Holy Spirit to guide and fill it, we may still use certain methods and techniques in prayer, just as we use standard forms of speech in everyday conversation. We simply keep in mind that the prayer method is not what causes the relationship with God any more than our speech patterns cause our friendships; it is simply a tool of communicating.

We can begin with a simple way to pray using Scripture developed by a Jesuit priest, Fr. Armand Nigro, SJ. I have been using it since I was a high school teacher back in 1972, and I still find it extremely useful, both personally and in the classroom. Fr. Nigro's "Five Ps of Prayer" are Place, Posture, Passage, Peace, and then back to the Passage. Let's go through each step.

A Place to Pray

We need a place of prayer that is quiet and free of disturbances and distractions. The prophet Elijah learned about the importance of silence on Mount Horeb, the mountain where God spoke with Moses. ("Mount Horeb" is the name for Mount Sinai in the northern Hebrew dialect.) God had appeared to Moses with smoke, cloud, thunder, and trumpet blasts. Elijah was fleeing from Queen Jezebel, who was trying to kill him, and he wanted the Lord to tell him why he, a prophet faithful to God's word and mission, was being persecuted. In response to that request, the Lord promised to pass by Elijah, just as he had done for Moses in Exodus 34:1-6. But God was neither in the strong wind and crushing rocks, nor in an earthquake, nor in a fire—manifestations that had occurred to Moses on the same mountain. Instead, God appeared in a small, whispering sound, with which he simply gave Elijah new instructions for his prophetic mission (1 Kings 19:1-18). Many people have learned from this episode that it is more likely that God will speak to us in a still, small voice than in the dramatic upheavals of nature.

> It is more likely that God will speak to us in a still, small voice.

If God's still, small voice is the experience of the vast majority of Christians, listening to him requires us to be quiet, interiorly and externally. Usually, before we find interior peace we need to seek out a quiet, peaceful, and religious place. By "religious," I mean a place that reminds us of the presence of God in a variety of ways.

My favorite places are chapels where the Blessed Sacrament is reserved, either in the tabernacle or exposed in a monstrance. Fortunately, a wave of Eucharistic adoration swept across the world in the period leading up to the 2000 Jubilee and since. This popular hunger for Eucharistic adoration has been nourished by the teaching and example of Pope John Paul II, the experience of Eucharistic congresses, as well as a movement urging pastors to make it possible for people to come sit or kneel before the Lord Jesus in the Blessed Sacrament. Some churches now offer Eucharistic adoration twenty-four hours a day, seven days a week. Many of the dioceses with frequent opportunities for Eucharistic adoration have seen an increase in vocations.

Over the centuries, Europeans have clearly understood the church as the central place of worship, but they have also extended the sacredness of the church to roadside and street-corner shrines. These shrines might consist of an icon of the Blessed Virgin or saint affixed to the exterior wall of a building or a crucifix along the road. Many Catholics in America do the same thing in their yards with shrines to the Sacred Heart of Jesus, Our Lady, St. Francis of Assisi, and other saints. When we cannot get to a Eucharistic chapel, we can pray in such places.

A further extension of sacred space can be made inside the home, with an area or a room set aside for prayer. Whenever a family member is in that area or room, the rest of the family will know that he or she is praying. Such a place may be adorned with a crucifix or other holy images of Jesus Christ, the Blessed Virgin, and some favorite saints. Perhaps even a candle or two will help remind us that this is a place set aside in our homes as an extension of the church into the home environment. Most of us religious and clergy are blessed to live in homes that have chapels set aside for quiet prayer and adoration. However we can accomplish this task, we should find a place to pray quietly and without distraction.

Posture

The second "P" refers to one's posture in prayer. No one posture is required during private prayer. This is not the case for the Church's public liturgical prayer, in which postures are prescribed in accord with the rubrics for each rite. At Mass, for example, there are set times to stand, genuflect, and kneel. However, in private prayer we may use any posture that keeps us both alert and relaxed. The goal in choosing a particular posture is to maintain that balance between peaceful listening to God and alertness.

Fr. Pedro Arrupe, SJ, a former Father General of the Jesuits, had been stationed in Japan for many years. While there, he learned to pray while standing on his head. I have never been able to stand on my head for *any* reason, let alone prayer. On the other hand, St. Ignatius of Loyola liked to pray lying down. If I were to do that, I would start meditating on the apostles in Gethsemane, to whom Jesus needed to ask, "Could you not stay awake with me even one hour?" (Matthew 26:40). That posture does not work for me any better than standing on my head. I have rheumatoid arthritis, so kneeling for a whole hour doesn't work for me any longer because the pain becomes too much of a distraction, as does the difficulty of getting off my knees.

The posture that works best for me is sitting still in a chair or pew. This is a very comfortable way to be attentive and listening. Other people kneel; some people lie prostrate before the Blessed Sacrament in adoration and worship, literally lowering themselves before God (the New Testament word translated as "worship" [*proskuneo*] means "to prostrate oneself"). I would suggest that each person experiment to find the posture that best suits him or her.

Choosing a Passage

The third "P" is the choosing of a passage from Scripture, which can be done in a wide variety of ways. Rather than using "Bible roulette," in which a person simply opens up the Bible at random and reads the first passage that catches the eye, it is better to have some kind of strategy for choosing a passage. As some people have learned, when you choose randomly, you eventually start finding passages with long lists of names. These are interesting to Bible geeks and may help you choose an ancient name for your child, but they are unlikely to advance your spiritual life.

> We Catholics are particularly blessed because we are nourished with so much Scripture in the liturgy.

One way to choose a passage is simply to use the daily or Sunday Mass readings. We Catholics are particularly blessed because we are nourished with so much Scripture in the liturgy. There are more than seven thousand Scripture verses in the three-year lectionary cycle for Sundays and another fourteen thousand verses in the two-year lectionary cycle for weekdays. We are meant not only to hear Scripture during the Holy Eucharist but to bring it back home for meditation and prayer. We can reflect and pray on these texts before we go to Mass on Sundays or on the weekdays, thereby praying through most of the Scriptures, especially the gospels and epistles.

This frequent and daily public reading of Scripture is an aid in making the Scriptures the very core of our prayer. It also nourishes our liturgical prayer, especially if we attend daily Mass.

Another plan for using the Mass readings might be to pray through all the gospel texts in one year, or through the daily responsorial psalms in a different year, or over several years to pray through the first readings. After taking three or four years to cover these texts, a person might be ready to start over with the first cycle of gospel texts. Since some of these readings are fairly long, one could extend this pattern of choosing Scripture readings for prayer and cover a lot of Scripture over the years of meditation.

A similar approach can be taken with the Liturgy of the Hours, which is the Church's official prayer book. This liturgy is required of priests and of many religious, but the laity are certainly invited and encouraged to pray it as well. Each day is divided into different times of prayer, with the goal of sanctifying the day. Each "hour" is structured around the psalms, with other readings included. The first hour of the day, the "Office of Readings," begins with three psalms and then includes a passage from Scripture and a selection from the writings of a saint or some official Church document. One could easily use these Scripture readings as the basis for a year's worth of meditations.

The psalms from any of the "hours" could be the passage chosen for private prayer. I focused on the psalms after my father and mother separated and divorced. Since many of the psalms are laments, as I prayed them, I allowed myself to prayerfully lament the breakup of my family. These laments express a wide range of emotions—weeping, anger, grief, frustration, loneliness—and yet are always based on an act of trust in God and his eventual salvation. Because of the power of these psalms of lamentation to express my own experience, I found them to be very helpful during this period of time.

Another plan is to take one of the gospels and pray through the whole book pericope by pericope. A pericope (a Greek word pronounced per-í-co-pee) is a set of verses that forms one coherent unit or thought, thus forming a short passage. Most Bibles mark out the pericopes with headings, letting you know when one section of sayings or one parable begins and ends. It is advisable to take no more than one pericope at a time, since it would be difficult to meditate on a passage that is too long. Trying to pray over too long a passage is like trying to eat a whole cake instead of just one slice.

Another simple and very useful way to choose a passage for prayer is to base your selection on the mysteries of the Rosary. There are many Scriptural Rosary pamphlets and books available that list one passage of Scripture for each Hail Mary for each of the twenty mysteries. This organization of texts—about two hundred verses in all—would cover multiple elements of the twenty most basic mysteries of the Christian faith. Such a program of choosing Bible passages for prayer would support the goals set out by Pope John Paul II in his apostolic letter *Rosarium Virginis Mariae* ("On the Most Holy Rosary"). He urged everyone to meditate more deeply on the mysteries of the Rosary, especially by using Scripture and by considering each mystery from the perspective of Our Lady, who looks at her Son with the special maternal love that she has for him. Such a plan of meditation would also enrich the way we pray the Rosary apart from those Scripture meditations, since meditation on the meaning of the mysteries is the very soul of the Rosary.

It is good to be aware of the variety of ways of choosing a passage from Scripture for prayer, but a key to using any of these methods is to choose the passage ahead of time rather than waiting until the actual time of prayer to start looking for a passage. By being prepared with a passage, one can start praying right away.

Approaching the Text in Prayer

The next step is simply that you pray. As stated earlier in this chapter, you must begin by asking the Holy Spirit to help and guide your prayer, since the same Holy Spirit who inspired these words of Scripture is also going to make it possible for the Scripture texts to speak to your heart and mind. Prayer is not a technique of human skills; it is part of your relationship with God, and only God can make this relationship come alive. For this reason, we depend on the help and inspiration of the Holy Spirit in our prayer.

In contrast to authentic Christian prayer, a person who tries to pray without the help of the Holy Spirit will merely try to think about and study the passages. Of course, it's good to do this. I do it professionally as a Scripture scholar. I examine points of grammar; I look up words and check out their roots in the original languages; I study the historical and cultural background. But this is not prayer. To be sure, scholarly research can be more than an academic exercise; it can inform and enrich our prayer. However, I must distinguish between the times when I'm sitting in the library looking up vocabulary and historical background and scholarly opinions and those occasions when I'm trying to listen to God speak. Listening to

God speak will be the central activity of our prayer. In order to hear the Lord address my heart and mind, I must depend on the Holy Spirit who inspired the sacred words of Scripture to stir within my heart.

There are many ways to approach the texts of Scripture in prayer. One of them in particular employs the imagination. As always, begin by asking the Holy Spirit for help. Then read the passage and imagine the scene being described in the text. For instance, you may decide to pray about Jesus' multiplication of the loaves and fishes. By imaginatively using your senses, picture the Sea of Galilee and the grassy place near the shore where, in fact, many large old trees grow. (The reason so many trees and so much grass grow is that seven springs of water come out of the ground there.) Imagine also with your sense of hearing: What would it sound like to be with five thousand men plus all the women and hungry children? What would it be like to hear the sea lapping on the shore and the voice of the Lord speaking to the crowd? Imagine even with your sense of taste: What would the barley bread taste like? What would the fish taste like? Would it be dried or smoked fish?

After you have used your imagination to picture the scene as vividly as possible, read the text again. Maybe certain phrases and words jump out at you, or perhaps a certain aspect of the scene recurs in your mind. As these things happen, consider that it is the Holy Spirit's doing, acting somewhat like a yellow high-lighter pen in your mind. You trusted him to help you in your prayer, but he is probably not going to speak in visions or audible voices. He doesn't really need to—he already inspired the word of God in Sacred Scripture, the guaranteed word of God.

As much as I have read the Bible—I've been reading it every day since I was a novice in 1968—and no matter how many times I have read particular texts or read or translated them from the original language, I am always amazed at new things that get the "yellow highlighter" treatment. Familiarity hardly breeds contempt. Familiarity with Scripture opens us up to amazing new insights and wisdom. Therefore, praying with the gospels by picturing the scenes and then reading over the texts lets the Holy Spirit highlight the message he has for a particular individual at a particular time in his or her life.

> Familiarity with Scripture opens us up to amazing new insights and wisdom.

What if we are not reading a gospel passage but are meditating on a text from St. Paul, a prophet, or some other text of Scripture? We may not have a concrete image around which we can develop our imagination. So what else can we do? St. Paul writes absolutely brilliant theology, so instead of using our imagination, approach it discursively. This approach recognizes the logic of each statement in the text. We can ask ourselves, "If these words of St. Paul are true, then what conclusions can I draw from them?" While our imagination is usually vivid and pictorial, our minds can use logic, taking one step after another and seeing where it leads. And that's another way we can meditate: Instead of picturing something in our imagination, we can take these steps of logic and see what flows from them. This can be another very powerful way to pray with Scripture texts outside the gospels or historical books.

Sensing the Spirit's Peace

The fourth "P" is peace. Once you sense the presence of the Holy Spirit, pause there and be at peace. Discover the peace that God bestows by his grace as we hear him speak to us. You may not get any new ideas—in fact, do not worry about getting new ideas. Rather, enjoy the sense of peace that St. Paul describes as "a peace that surpasses understanding" (Philippians 4:7). Instead of worrying about gaining new insights into the text, simply allow the Holy Spirit to fill your heart with his peace in connection with a certain line or word or passage, and rest in that quiet.

For most of us, depending on what stage of development we find ourselves in our prayer life, that peace will eventually begin to fade. For this reason, the fifth "P" involves returning to the passage and seeking the peace of the Holy Spirit again. You keep going back and forth, to the passage and then to the peace, until you finish your time of prayer.

It is good to set a predetermined period of time for your prayer rather than praying until you feel like stopping. Perhaps consider our Lord's suggestion: "Could you not spend an hour with me?" (see Matthew 26:40). That may seem like a long time because we all have a lot to do. Yet we might learn from St. Francis de Sales' conversation with the mayor of his town, who said, "You know, Bishop Francis, I can't spend an hour in prayer. I've got so much to do." Francis responded, "Anyone as busy as you are needs two hours of prayer!"

A surprising result of taking a regular, predetermined, and suitably long amount of time for prayer is that we will probably get more done than if we did not pray. This is an act of faith, but it almost seems as if God multiplies our minutes when we give him a decent amount of prayer time. An Old Testament norm may be useful here: Give a tithe, that is, 10 percent of your day for prayer, including Mass, perhaps the Liturgy of the Hours, the Rosary, and meditation. This may be difficult at the outset, so it is a good idea to start out in smaller chunks of time. Babies do not start off running; they crawl and then take baby steps. So also with prayer—one can begin with small steps but keep in view a good long run as the goal. Just as we need exercise to maintain our body's physical health, so do we need prayer to maintain our spiritual and moral health. Some people even combine physical and spiritual exercise. I like to pray my Rosary as I walk. Others want to keep each of these activities separate and distinct. Do whatever helps you to keep praying sufficiently.

What if we don't feel God's peace in prayer, even when we are doing everything that we should? One reason we may not feel that peace is because there is some area of sin in our lives that we have not brought before the Lord and need to confess—especially if it's serious sin that needs to be confessed to a priest. So when we aren't feeling peace in our prayer, we should examine our consciences, especially for areas that we may be avoiding or neglecting. Such an examination may take a significant amount of time, especially if we have neglected that component of prayer in the past. However, it is a very important step toward spiritual progress and so should not be a cause of discouragement.

Perhaps in our examination we discover an area of sin that we have not even noticed before because it is so much a part of the normal, everyday pattern of our lives. For instance, maybe we aren't treating our spouses, children, or parents as kindly as we should. Maybe we are gossiping on a regular basis. When we have trouble discovering such weaknesses, we should ask the people we live with how they view our behavior. They may welcome the opportunity to tell us—and we should listen to what they have to say! Not only family members but also a spiritual director can help you. And if you can't find a spiritual director, you might find a good friend who you can talk to about your life.

Another reason for not feeling peace may have nothing to do with any moral failures on our part. Quite possibly we need to mature in our spiritual life, and the Lord withdraws his peace as a way to encourage us to grow. At times he seems to withdraw somewhat until we step out to find him. If he does not withdraw his peace and consolation, we might easily become complacent about our present state of spiritual development. However, it is important to realize that the withdrawal of peace is not always a punishment but a loving way to motivate us to grow.

I like to think of the way God prods us to maturity in the same way that I helped my little brother learn to walk. Just before I turned fourteen, my brother, Jimmy, was born. I spent a lot of time with my baby brother, including teaching him how to walk. I would let him grab my fingers with his hands, raise his hands above his head, and lead him to walk a few steps. Then I would pull my hands away from his fingers. He would gasp, take a step or two on his own, and then grab onto my finger again. We would repeat this game, and he would laugh and do it again and again until he finally learned how to walk on his own. Sometimes our Lord trains us to walk spiritually. He lets us hold his finger, figuratively speaking, by granting us gifts of peace and letting us take baby steps of spiritual growth. Then he withdraws the peace the way I pulled back my fingers from my brother, in order to let us take a few steps on our own so that we build up our spiritual muscles. Perhaps we gasp out of fear: "Where are you, Lord?" But we need to take those steps to move closer to him. God wants us to reach deeper levels of spiritual development, even when we think we are not ready. God thinks we are ready, and so he helps us to grow. Just keep in mind that the goal of our prayer is to find true peace with God; he intends to restore us to his peace, probably sooner rather than later. Do not fear the lack of peace, but learn from it, and mature in prayer.

To sum up, if I don't feel God's peace in my prayer time, the first step I take is to examine my conscience. Am I offending others, or do I need to change in some way? Is there something I can do about it? Second, if I don't find anything that offends my conscience, then I consider asking the Lord, "Where do you want me to go? What's the next stage?" We can listen to his response as we continue to follow him each day.

This "five Ps" method of prayerfully listening to God is simply one way to pray; there are many others that have been very useful to people. However, this is a good way to begin praying with Scripture. Further growth and deepening of the relationship with God will lead you to search for other methods of prayer. Use them to the extent they help you in coming close to God. Yet always keep in mind that prayer is a gift of God's grace. Depend on him for that gift as you continually seek to listen to him.

Questions for Reflection and Discussion

1. How often do you pray the Scriptures? Do you see Scripture as a way for God to speak to you? Why or why not?

2. Where do you usually pray? Is it an environment that is conducive to hearing God? Where else might you go that would help you to hear God?

3. How does your posture influence your prayer? Are there times when kneeling or prostrating yourself might be appropriate or help you to better focus?

4. Do you choose a passage to pray before you come to prayer? Are there favorite passages to which you return again and again?

5. How often do you experience God's peace when you pray? If you are not feeling his peace, do you try to determine why?

CHAPTER 7

A BALANCING ACT

Integrating Our Intellect, Emotions, and Will

Discerning God's will is not an experience of warm and fuzzy feelings. Rather, it means recognizing and choosing things that are good in themselves and are the good things that God wants us to do. In our discernment process, we need balance, and we can achieve this by integrating our intellect, our will, and our emotions into our prayer and discernment. All three are necessary to discern God's will properly. Each one in isolation can be inadequate for the task. As we move forward in this process and get insights in prayer, we also need to grow in humility so that we remain balanced and open to the insights and graces that others receive.

OUR INTELLECT

Some religious people view the role of the intellect in the spiritual life with suspicion. They may be reacting to the fact that some theologians seem to exclude their faith in their studies and come up with stunning conclusions, such as denying the virgin birth or the resurrection. But that doesn't mean that we should avoid the study of theology. Rather, we can seek a way to integrate the intellect into our faith life and allow our minds to help guide us in listening to God.

It's clear that Scripture itself attributes a positive role to the mind and its ability to gain wisdom. Proverbs, Sirach, and Wisdom, as well as Job and Ecclesiastes, are all books dedicated to attaining wisdom. Many other books, particularly the psalms but also some episodes in the historical narratives and in the prophets, contain elements of wisdom teaching. In Scripture, wisdom is often personified as a lady who invites people to forsake folly. Wisdom is also presented in proverbs and other instructions as something attainable for anyone who is willing to think about life and its quandaries.

The topics treated in the wisdom literature are quite varied: respect for parents, honesty in business, concern about working hard in order to eat, relationships between spouses, the discipline of children, and the relationship between kings and subjects. Sirach even addresses a variety of professions, including the only extensive treatment of medical doctors in the Bible (38:1-15). A typical proverb says, "Treasures gained by wickedness do not profit, but righteousness delivers from death" (Proverbs 10:2). Notice that the verse does not advise the reader to take any specific action; it simply states a fact about the difference between wicked and righteous wealth. The reader must then think about what this means and draw his or her own conclusions, which requires thinking and reflection.

At this very basic level, we can see that the use of human reason is assumed to be the way to gain insight into the proverb. This assumption permeates all of the wisdom literature, thereby encouraging careful thought. If this is the case, then it is wise to apply the use of our minds throughout life, thinking carefully and reflecting well.

Yet note that one of the basic and explicitly mentioned principles of using the mind is to begin with faith in God. In fact, the introduction to Proverbs says, "The beginning of knowledge is fear of the LORD" (Proverbs 1:7). This principle is restated in Proverbs 9:10, Psalm 111:10, Job 28:28, and Ecclesiastes 12:13. The reason some scholars allow their learning to lead them away from their faith is that they do not let the fear of the Lord guide their intellectual pursuits. Remember that any and every intellectual study has a starting point, a basic assumption upon which the rest of the ideas are built, like the ground on which a building is constructed. If the ground is weak and muddy, then the building will not stand, as Jesus taught at the end of the Sermon on the Mount (Matthew 7:24-27). If the ground or starting point for the mind's investigation of God and theology is based on faith, then the building will be strong and will be a shelter for those who enter it.

> Starting with faith, reason can build and develop one's ability to listen to God and follow him well.

Starting with faith, reason can build and develop one's ability to listen to God and follow him well. The mind uses some basic simple tools. The most basic is the principle of noncontradiction, the principle upon which all logic is founded. This principle holds that something cannot be true and untrue at the same time; a particular thing cannot be that thing and at the same time and in the same way be that thing. One of the most important structures of logic is the syllogism. This is a general statement that begins with a major premise. For instance, all dogs are mammals. The minor premise, dealing with a specific thing, could be that my pet Fido is a dog. Therefore, one can draw a conclusion: Fido is a mammal. Of course, syllogisms can become quite complex, and people can argue about the proper application of the rules of logic in any specific case, or they might argue whether the major and minor premises are true. Those points are precisely what make an argument educational, challenging, and even fun.

These are among some of the rich tools that reason can employ in making sense of various ideas. St. Thomas Aquinas was brilliant in the way he stated the propositions of the Christian faith, then listed all the objections he could find, and finally answered each objection in sequence. His mind was able to bring clarity to many of the most profound mysteries of the Christian faith, which is why so many people have continued to study his works over the past eight hundred years.

When it comes to God's revelation, we would do well to deduce conclusions about its meaning through thoughtful reflection. We can ask: "What does this passage mean? What did it mean to the ancient people who first heard it? How might their ancient yet still very human circumstance relate to my own? How, then, do I apply the passage to my life?" This kind of reflection is a dialogue with the texts of Scripture, a drawing out of the meaning from the texts. When this is done, we have more information and understanding to bring to our prayer time, a time in which we invite the Lord to address our own life with the message of his word. The process of thinking and deducing is not the same as praying; however, such reflection on revelation will augment our prayer.

One caution can be made in regard to the use of our intellect. A Christian may think deeply and carefully about God's word. The assumptions may be based on faith and the truth of the Church's revelation. A great deal of knowledge may be present in the mind, yet another quality might still be missing. In addition to knowledge in the head, there is a need for God's grace to stoke a fire of love for him in our hearts. If the well-trained, orthodox believer is to make an impact in the lives and souls of his hearers, then the commitment to a deep prayer life is absolutely necessary. The correct and true words of doctrine can flame into an enthusiasm to evangelize, teach, and serve others only if the heart remains open to the action of the Holy Spirit, who draws us to know and

> The process of thinking and deducing is not the same as praying; however, such reflection on revelation will augment our prayer.

love Jesus Christ and in him to hallow the Father's name and love him with all that we are.

The same St. Thomas Aquinas who brilliantly explained the faith in his *Summa Theologica* and his Scripture commentaries was later heard to say that this brilliance was straw in comparison to the intense gift of knowing God in profound prayer. Based on his personal devotion, he was also capable of writing magnificent hymns that are still sung today, like the *Pange Lingua*. His heart could soar when writing hymns, and he was most famous among his contemporaries for the many sermons that moved his congregations to deep devotion. The reason that people could respond to his words was due not merely to the clarity of his thought. Rather, a deep prayer life allowed the truths of the faith, which he expressed so well in his writings on theology, to work within his spirit as well as in his mind. St. Thomas' prayerful listening to God in regard to the deep mysteries of the faith gave his words a resonance of truth and authenticity and evoked a response of faith from his hearers.

We, too, can learn from St. Thomas about the spiritual life. We study our faith; we learn as much theology as we are capable of; we read, reflect, and engage in logical discourse with friends and foes alike. Yet for all the great good this does, we still need to spend time before Christ in prayer. We listen to him speak to our hearts and spirits the truths of our faith. In them we hear Jesus Christ speaking to us because we allow the Holy Spirit to stir us interiorly. Through all this we cannot help but grow in a deeper love of God.

OUR EMOTIONS

Observing the movements of our soul, as outlined by St. Ignatius in his Rules for the Discernment of Spirits, is an important part of the discernment process. We need to be aware of our emotions because they may indicate to us what kinds of influences are acting upon us. However, when we rely solely on our emotions and instincts to guide us, we can be led down the wrong path.

For example, there have been many individuals who have claimed to be visionaries who see apparitions of Mary and receive messages from her. It takes the Church a long time to verify such claims, but sometimes people are so touched by these messages that they don't want to look closely at them to determine if they are valid or in line with Church teaching. In another example of our emotions leading us astray, in the late 1960s, people wanted Mass to "feel" more relevant, so much experimentation went on—leading to various liturgical abuses that have thankfully dwindled since then.

Emotions may well come into play during our prayer, but emotion on its own can never provide a solid basis for discernment. Human feelings change far too easily and arbitrarily—just look at the teenager who falls in love one day and out of love the next. We would do well to accept the fact that our emotions change as rapidly as the state of our health, the weather, or even the freshness of our food. This is an aspect of human nature we can all live with if we keep our feelings in perspective. We can enjoy

> The emotions have an important role in helping the will.

the good feelings and try not to sweat the negative ones, but we should always move forward on the basis of good solid thinking and reflection.

Keep in mind, however, that this does not mean that we exclude the emotions. The emotions do have an important role in helping the will. Even when the mind makes clear which choice is the best, and even when a prayerful meditation becomes a grace in which we understand what God wants us to do—even when we say yes to all this—there is still a useful role for the emotions. Just as diesel oil fuels a locomotive climbing up a mountain grade, emotions fuel our motivation. Our feelings of fear, urgency, tender attraction to someone, compassion for a weak person, and all the other wonderful or frightening emotions we might experience can help us stick to the decisions we have made through the will. We may feel daunted by the task ahead of us, but we keep moving forward like a committed football team on a long drive to the goal line. Even what we consider the "negative" emotions can sometimes be helpful; for example, we may be afraid to give up on ourselves or our decisions.

At times each of us will have to force ourselves to do that which is good but difficult. We will make great and at times even heroic efforts to perform acts that are superior to those that "feels good" at the moment. Ask the alcoholic who has resisted the one drink that would lead him back into addiction. Ask the college student who may have felt like staying in bed instead of going to class. Life is replete with such examples, and every one of us can look back—usually not too far into our past—to recollect such events.

At the same time, some feelings may change and urge us to give up or quit. At those times we need to remind ourselves of the decisions we made, the acts of our will to accomplish the good that God desires of us. We may need to dig more deeply within ourselves to stay motivated. However, as we make that decision to keep going, we will tap into still deeper emotions to fuel our efforts. We may even tap into a deep determination that is based on anger, which is the emotion that confronts failure and frustration. Tapping into that deep anger—not the superficiality of mere whining—can drive us to complete nearly impossible tasks set before us by God. Perhaps that is why St. Paul cites Psalm 4:4 when he exhorts us Christians to "be angry, but sin not" (Ephesians 4:26). In so doing, we will find that fidelity to the acts of the will, which our minds have clearly and faithfully set before us, are driven to completion by the deepest of feelings and loves.

OUR WILL

The balance and integration of rational thinking with human feeling in our prayer life will help us discern God's will better than if we used these wonderful gifts in a disordered way. However, one more component needs to be integrated—the will. The will is that aspect of human personality by which we choose to take certain actions. Our will makes decisions and then strengthens us to stick to them. Of course, the will cannot know what these choices are unless thinking and reflection on the various possibilities take place first. Our minds take in information on the possibilities in front of us. Our reason analyzes each possibility, asking, "What will work? Why will it work? Can I do this?" We go through this process every time we buy a car, choose a school, or decide what to eat for lunch. On all levels of life, we try to learn what our options are, and we rationally think about each one. Without the use of our reason, we could not weigh the advantages and disadvantages of each option.

Certainly there are some people who want to be spontaneous and simply "go with the flow" without a lot of thought beforehand. But the fact is that the intellect, not spontaneous emotion, is what makes free will possible. Each person can know and understand the available choices in life. Then that person can make a choice, and with it a commitment. Good decision making is the core of human freedom.

Remember that freedom of the will is not the be-all and end-all of life. Various existentialist philosophers denied that life had any meaning except for the ability to make free choices. Rather, we Christians have heard incredibly good news that God not only exists but that he loves each person and invites each person to choose to accept that love. Everyone can study Scripture and Church teaching, and everyone can weigh the merits of the faith by thinking and reflecting on it. However, at some point we exercise our free will by accepting God's grace of faith. We not only believe his truths in our minds, but we also make a commitment to him and choose to be faithful to him. This means that simply being free and having free will is not the highest good of human existence. Rather, the highest choice of our will is to make the choice to love God and follow him throughout this life and into eternal life. It leads not to meaninglessness but to eternal life in heaven, loving and being loved for all eternity.

Humility

Humility is also important if we are to achieve balance in our discernment process. One possible consequence of getting new insights and consolations in prayer is to think that everyone else should have the same experiences. Many novitiates in religious orders have this problem, but it could apply to many new members of prayer groups or lay movements. We may be tempted to adopt the "only this" or "this alone" mentality and think that our own insights from Scripture and our own methods and styles of prayer are for everyone and are the only way to God.

How do we combat this tendency? Humility requires that we accept the fact that there are many ways to pray and that there are multiple insights we can get from Scripture, since many layers of understanding still remain in the text. We would do well to remain open to everything that the Holy Spirit offers in revelation, whether these truths eventually impinge on our lives or not. We humbly accept that other people may receive other insights, and perhaps we will not.

Furthermore, we may have heard an authentic truth from God during prayer, but that insight and wisdom are not necessarily meant for everyone else. If our Lord gives us a great insight or consolation, that fact does not necessarily mean that we must tell others about it or that we must claim to have received spe-

> We humbly accept that other people may receive other insights, and perhaps we will not.

cial locutions and messages for the world. Perhaps I am the only person who needs to hear the word God has given. Also, it is possible that we have misunderstood some point in Scripture, and our insight is theologically faulty or flat-out wrong. We should never share error with anyone else, and we would do well to forget about it ourselves. How, when, where, with whom, and if we share these insights are thing we must also discern.

Perhaps in prayer we are so taken by one aspect of our faith that we are tempted to ignore or downplay the others. For example, some have so emphasized the divine embrace of human nature in the Incarnation that they neglect the reality of original sin. The genius of Catholicism is its ability to maintain all of the truths of the faith and celebrate each of them. The liturgical year helps us maintain this balance. We start the year with the season of Advent, when we remember the longing of Israel for God's redemption. In the Christmas season, we celebrate the Word made flesh. In Lent we recall the need to repent of sin as we meditate on the sufferings of Christ and his death on the cross. After fasting from the good things of this world, we celebrate the glorious feasts of Easter and Pentecost. This balance of celebrations shapes the way we see the world throughout the year.

Religious orders and lay movements in the Church often highlight one or another aspect of the life of Jesus or the gospel. Various founders may have felt compelled to spotlight certain doctrines, especially in those times in history when there was a tendency to neglect those truths. For example, the Passionists emphasize Christ's passion in their spiritual life and preaching, while the Precious Blood religious emphasize the power of Christ's redeeming blood. All such orders and congregations coexist within the Church. Each one focuses on one aspect of Catholic truth but does not deny the reality of all aspects of the faith. Each order simply allows its emphasis to emerge and remain integral to Catholic life.

As we begin hearing God in prayer, we must also accept the fact that we do not deserve the incredible graces our Lord has bestowed on us. Humility includes openness to any of the further graces our Lord might bestow. Equally important is the ability to accept the wonderful graces our Lord might bestow on other people, especially if these graces seem greater than the ones we have received. Some people have more natural talents than we do, and some have more supernatural spiritual gifts. Any feelings of envy or jealousy will only feed the sin of pride. We should not put ourselves down or claim to be nothing, since this can still be a way to focus on ourselves. Rather, we rejoice that others have these gifts. We are delighted that they are blessed with gifts that we may neither have nor understand. We praise and glorify God for his generosity to others, which then keeps our attention on what God is doing rather than on what we are doing.

Humility also recognizes that I am not the touchstone of truth, and therefore I must look to the Church. We do not accept insights that are inconsistent with the Church's teachings. A humble person accepts willingly the correction of any error or false element in his insights, even if the insights are received in prayer.

Furthermore, we accept those teachings of Scripture and the Church that we do not yet understand or that we have not personally received in prayer. It is a profound act of pride to reject the truths taught by the Church and Scripture over the centuries

> Humility also recognizes that I am not the touchstone of truth, and therefore I must look to the Church.

just because we do not understand them. Rather, we accept them, we pray that we may gain insight and understanding, and we wait for the time when we might receive that insight—if we ever do receive it in this life. One way in which humility affects our attitude toward listening to God is the realization that I may never know certain things, maybe because they are none of my business or maybe because I do not have the mental or spiritual capacity to grasp them. We may be open to learning more and gaining new insight, but I can be quite comfortable with not needing to know everything; that is God's job, and it is in his capacity alone.

We need the one Church that Christ founded to be that "pillar and bulwark of truth" (1 Timothy 3:15). We learn from her history that many sinners have lived in the Church, some who repented and reformed their lives and some who did not. We seek to imitate the holy and wise members of the Church while at the same time recognizing that each one of us could fall into the same sins as others who have been baptized over the centuries. With such a perspective, we can proceed to accept the various insights God bestows on us and enjoy the wonderful fruits of our prayer life.

Questions for Reflection and Discussion

1. How often do you study and reflect on the truths of the faith? How do you see such a practice enriching your prayer life?

2. How can you guard against letting your emotions lead you astray, especially spiritually?

3. What is the link between decision making and human freedom? Why do we feel more free when we make good decisions?

4. Why is it important that we use our intellect, our emotions, and our will in our discernment process? What happens when one is missing?

5. Do you listen to God with an attitude of humility? How can you prevent yourself from falling into the "only my way is best" mentality?

CHAPTER 8

LISTENING TO GOD IN DIFFICULT TIMES

Seeing the Big Picture

Our willingness to listen to God and our attentiveness to him in prayer will mean that we experience more peace and joy, not just while we are praying, but especially as our prayer becomes more deeply integrated with the rest of our lives. Regularly examining our consciences gives us an increased awareness of the need to repent of our sins—sins we may not have even noticed before we looked to Jesus Christ as our model and goal—and the fruit of this practice will also bring us peace and joy.

Yet this increase of peace and joy and even, dare we say it, holiness does not mean that we will float through life on a cloud, untouched by its pain, failures, and disappointments. We need to be alert to hearing God speak, not only in the highs of religious peace and external success, but also in the struggles and problems of life.

The story of Joseph (Genesis 37, 39–50), one of the longest narratives in the Old Testament, shows how God used this man to save his whole family—yet this happened only through a series of painful events. At first Joseph is clearly favored by God and by his father, Jacob. Special clothes from his father accompany special dreams from God, dreams that indicate that Joseph will one day rule over his older bothers. Rather than accepting these dreams as God's will, the brothers sell Joseph into slavery, which was one small step above their original plan to kill him. As a slave in Egypt, Joseph advances quite well in the household of Potiphar —too well, it seems. Potiphar's wife tries to seduce him but fails because Joseph is too virtuous to sin against his master. This virtue is rewarded by the woman's accusations of rape, followed by Joseph's imprisonment. While in prison, he correctly interprets the dreams of two royal officials, Pharaoh's chief baker and his cup-bearer. A considerable time later, the royal cup-bearer introduces Joseph to Pharaoh, who has been deeply disturbed by two dreams of his own. Joseph's interpretation of seven years of plentiful crops followed by seven years of severe famine comes true, so he is appointed the Grand Vizier of Egypt, second only to Pharaoh. During the seven years of famine, Joseph's brothers come to him seeking food, bowing down to him in accord with his boyhood dreams about them. They do not recognize him, but finally he reveals himself, is reconciled, and again sees his father, Jacob.

None of this would have happened if the brothers had not sold Joseph into slavery. Nor would his rise to power have occurred unless he had been falsely accused of rape and jailed with the palace officials. Had he not been in jail, he would not have been in the position to ration food through the seven years of famine and save his own family as well as the Egyptians. Joseph was eventually able to see God's plan, as he proclaimed to his brothers in Genesis 45:5-8:

And now do not be distressed, or angry with yourselves, because you sold me here; for God sent me before you to preserve life. For the famine has been in the land these two years; and there are yet five years in which there will be neither plowing nor harvest. And God sent me before you to preserve for you a remnant on earth, and to keep alive for you many survivors. So it was not you who sent me here, but God; and he has made me a father to Pharaoh, and lord of all his house and ruler over all the land of Egypt.

A Larger Plan

We would do well to read the whole story in Genesis, since it is so well written. The actual texts bring out important and wonderful details that our summary necessarily omits. Each of us can listen to the story of Joseph and learn to see God acting through the difficult situations and episodes of our owns lives, knowing that a much larger plan may be unfolding—larger than we can imagine at the present moment.

I have learned this lesson in many ways, both big and small. As a novice, for example, I got into a lot of arguments, mostly because I did not know enough to defend my opinions; my tenacity often yielded to stubbornness. This was remedied by correction from my friends as well as a better study of the English language and the acquiring of facts rather than my relying on mere instincts. I never enjoyed the embarrassment I felt at being corrected, but I certainly learned a lot from it.

A far greater crisis occurred while I was working with kids in a Chicago street gang in 1970. My friend Jimmy and I were attacked. One of the assailants beat me up. The other two made Jimmy kneel down, and then they shot him through the head.

Jimmy was a former gang member who had turned his life around and was planning to get married. He had asked me to bring him and his girlfriend to a priest for confession just two weeks before he was killed. My efforts in the neighborhood came to a terrible end with his murder. For me, this tragedy was followed by nightly dreams of being chased by people trying to kill me. My attempts to use a method of dream analysis to overcome these nightmares merely drew me into the New Age movement for a while. I finally experienced an emotional healing while watching a movie in which a man was murdered in the same way as Jimmy. Following the movie I cried very bitterly, an emotional catharsis that ended the nightmares.

The spiritual healing occurred still later when the spiritual director of my annual retreat assigned me to pray over this passage from Isaiah (43:1-4):

> But now thus says the LORD, he who created you, O Jacob,
>> he who formed you, O Israel:
> "Fear not, for I have redeemed you;
>> I have called you by name, you are mine.
> When you pass through the waters, I will be with you;
>> and through the rivers, they shall not overwhelm you;
> when you walk through fire you shall not be burned,
>> and the flame shall not consume you.
> For I am the LORD your God,
>> the Holy One of Israel, your Savior.
> I give Egypt as your ransom,
>> Ethiopia and Seba in exchange for you.
> Because you are precious in my eyes,

and honored, and I love you,
  I give men in return for you,
    peoples in exchange for your life. (RSV)

For two days, five hours a day, I meditated on this passage, taking those truths spoken to Israel during its exile in Babylon and applying them to myself. Step-by-step I came to accept the fact that the Lord had created and formed me, even with my limitations. The same Lord saves us from various kinds of dangers. Israel passed through raging rivers and blazing fires when it was destroyed by Babylon; the return to the homeland promised more of the same. I looked back on the seventeen gang fights that I tried to stop during my novitiate year at Holy Family Parish. Two times people fired pistols at me; other times bricks and bottles flew; twice gangs of girls tried to tear each other apart with a fury in their eyes that frightened me more than the boys with their weapons. Once I helped save a boy from being stabbed by a drunk, but the angry glance from the man with the knife indicated that suddenly my own life was at risk. My safety and life had been threatened precisely because I was trying to serve our Lord in a poor area of Chicago in response to the call that I heard during those days and hours of prayer in my novitiate.

Pain Becomes Part of Our Prayer

Being prayerful in difficult situations does not always take the pain away or resolve the situation. While I was working on my doctorate at Vanderbilt, I came home on Father's Day for a surprise visit to my family. But I was the one who was surprised when

I learned that my father had left my mother for another woman. Naturally, I was furious and my heart broke, yet I kept bringing the situation to prayer. Each day as I prayed the Liturgy of the Hours, the psalms came alive for me, particularly the psalms of lament. I related easily to the psalmist's outrage, his pleading for help, and his professions of faith, all mixed together in the laments. Then, while I was in the midst of two days of exams, Dad informed me that he had filed for divorce, just days before their wedding anniversary on the following Sunday.

That weekend I had to celebrate five Masses, and the gospel reading for that Sunday was Mark 10:2-12, a passage in which Jesus prohibits divorce. As I preached against divorce and talked about God's plan for the stability of marriage and the family, I avoided looking at any faces in the congregation because if I had, I would have burst into tears. Yet it was precisely that pain in my chest that I brought to the bread and wine when I lifted them up at the offertory. I trusted that just as Jesus would consecrate the bread and wine, so would he consecrate my grief over the breakup of my family. Somehow, I believed, God would bring good out of the situation and eventually lead my parents to reconcile with each other. That reconciliation did not happen the way I desired it, which would have been in time to stop my dad from leaving home. However, it did occur a few years later when Mom was in the last month of her life, dying of cancer; they kissed and said to each other, "I love you." Keep in mind that I had been praying throughout the years of their separation. The pain evoked by the family breakup did not go away as a result of my praying; rather, it became an integral aspect of my prayer.

Being prayerful does not mean that you or your loved ones will never get sick. I came down with rheumatoid arthritis when I turned forty. Certainly I asked God to heal me of this disease, since it has been debilitating at times. However, the discovery of new treatments has been as much an answer to my prayers as a complete cure would be. Furthermore, I was able to participate in clinical trials for these treatments, and I view my participation as a service to others who have the disease. I also thank God that I live at a time when such diseases can be treated; had I contracted it fifty years earlier, I would have become an invalid.

I find it better to listen to God through the midst of the difficulties rather than telling God that there are better ways he could run the universe.

Even recently, while writing this book, I contracted shingles—two months before I would have turned sixty, when I could have gotten the shingles vaccine. But these situations are part of life. Never do I find it helpful to ask, "Why me? Why did this happen to me?" It is especially unhelpful when the question is a rhetorical way of saying to God, "You should never have let me suffer. What's wrong with you, Lord?" If I ask why a problem comes my way, it is better to ask it in a prayerful way: "Lord, what do you want me to do in this situation? What is the mission you have in store for me now? Is there some person, perhaps a doctor, nurse, or patient, whom you want me to talk to? Do you want to use the situation to help me introduce someone else to you? What is your will in this?" Of course, in the difficulties I have mentioned, it may be relatively easy to take such an attitude; these are not life-threatening sicknesses, nor are they as painful and frightening as are many other illnesses. However, a self-pity that exaggerates our problems does no one any good. I find it better to listen to God through the midst of the difficulties rather than telling God that there are better ways he could run the universe, at least as it affects me and my well-being.

To people who pray, it may seem like a failure of faith when they experience pain, problems, and suffering in their lives, because they expect God to prevent such problems for the people he loves. However, he does allow such things to happen to the people he loves, from his Son Jesus Christ to the greatest sinner among us. But when we recognize the good things that are accomplished in these difficult situations, we will be better able to listen to God in the midst of them.

The Perspective of Scripture

Although our prayer life may not have prevented us from having the problem, it will help us see it within the perspective of God's revelation by reading and reflecting on Scripture. Our natural reactions to life's problems and tragedies are simply that —natural and therefore common to all people. We all get frustrated, angry, and depressed; some people become hopeless and despairing. We do not easily see beyond the pain. Joseph in the Book of Genesis did not rage against God when he was in trouble, but some Old Testament saints did. The prophet Jeremiah bitterly complained to God when his own relatives tried to kill him, but the Lord responded to the complaint this way:

"If you have raced with men on foot, and
    they have wearied you,
  how will you compete with horses?
And if in a safe land you fall down,
  how will you do in the jungle of the Jordan?"
    (Jeremiah 12:5, RSV)

In other words, "You ain't seen nothin' yet, kid; your trials are going to multiply." Jeremiah's bitterness builds until it culminates in this outburst:

"O LORD, you deceived me,
  and I was deceived;
you are stronger than I,
  and you have prevailed.
I have become a laughingstock all the day;
  every one mocks me." (20:7, RSV)

Jeremiah's accusation against God is quite strong because he has been arrested and put into the stocks like a criminal, precisely because he was faithful to proclaiming the word God had given to him. However, despite his frustration, he proclaims his trust in God:

"But the LORD is with me as a dread warrior;
  therefore my persecutors will stumble,
  they will not overcome me.
They will be greatly shamed,
  for they will not succeed.

Their eternal dishonor
    will never be forgotten." (20:11, RSV)

At the same time, he expresses grief that he was ever born to see such misery:

Cursed be the day
    on which I was born!
The day when my mother bore me,
    let it not be blessed!
Cursed be the man
    who brought the news to my father,
"A son is born to you,"
    making him very glad.
Let that man be like the cities
    which the LORD overthrew without pity;
let him hear a cry in the morning
    and an alarm at noon,
because he did not kill me in the womb;
    so my mother would have been my grave,
    and her womb for ever great.
Why did I come forth from the womb
    to see toil and sorrow,
    and spend my days in shame? (20:14-18, RSV)

We can also reflect on the story of Jonah, who was called by God to preach in Nineveh, the capital of the Assyrian empire. In those times the Assyrians were famous for their cruelty to enemies. Imagine if God had commanded a rabbi in Russia to go to Berlin during World War II to warn the Nazis that their city would be destroyed in three days unless they repented of their sins. A sensible rabbi might catch the next train to Siberia rather than try to make Hitler and the Nazis repent in sackcloth and ashes. Jonah took off in the opposite direction of God's call, but he was thwarted by a tremendous storm. He told the sailors that he was the reason for the storm threatening to destroy their ship and their lives, and he asked them to toss him overboard, perhaps as a better alternative to preaching in Nineveh. Then after being swallowed by a great fish, he prayed:

> "For you cast me into the deep,
>   into the heart of the seas,
>   and the flood was round about me;
> all your waves and your billows
>   passed over me.
> The waters closed in over me,
>   the deep was round about me;
> weeds were wrapped about my head
>   at the roots of the mountains.
> I went down to the land
>   whose bars closed upon me for ever;
> yet you brought up my life from the Pit,
>   O Lord my God." (Jonah 2:3-6, RSV)

Jonah did go back to Nineveh, where he preached with such success that even the animals fasted and wore sackcloth and ashes. But Jonah became furious with God because his mission to Nineveh was so successful. We can imagine the rabbi of our previous example preaching so successfully to the Nazis that they thoroughly repent and receive God's forgiveness. Those people had wreaked havoc on Europe, particularly on the Jews; he would want to see them annihilated for their crimes, and yet God dares to forgive them. Similarly, Jonah wanted to witness the thorough destruction of the wicked people of his own day, and he became angry that God had mercy on them. How dare God be so merciful! So Jonah pouted before the Lord until he learned a lesson from a simple plant (Jonah 4).

Our problems may be very big; they may cause pain beyond that which we can understand. However, we would do well to listen to God speaking to us in these episodes of the great prophets. We may try to imagine all that Jeremiah and Jonah were going through. How might they have felt in their circumstances? Have I ever experienced problems similar to theirs? How can I make their prayers and laments my own, adapting them to my particular circumstance? How would the Lord speak to me, given the way I react to the pain in my life? What might our Lord say to me when I complain like Jeremiah or pout like Jonah? Praying over these texts may help me hear God address me in my pain, which will take me much further than mere complaints ever could.

Seeing Our Suffering through Christ's Passion and Death

However, we can go to deeper levels of hearing God in our trials than the Old Testament prophets Jonah and Jeremiah are capable of showing us. This is possible if we listen to God speaking to us through the experience of Jesus Christ; that is, we can learn to see our suffering through Christ's passion and death, and find not only deeper understanding but healing as well.

One evening at a First Friday Mass for the charismatic prayer groups of the San Diego diocese, I preached a sermon on the way the Lord may call us to do things we would rather not do. After Mass I went to the back of the church to meditate on the readings for the following Sunday. I was in the quiet dark of the peaceful church when a woman from one of the prayer teams approached to ask me if I would mind helping her pray for the sick. Frankly I did mind; I wanted to pray privately. But since I had just preached a long sermon about doing the ministry we would rather not do, I felt I had to acquiesce. When I arrived at the sanctuary, the leader for the evening asked if I would lead the group in a healing prayer, since there were too many people there to pray for each person individually. With a sigh and a wry smile, I agreed. This was one evening in which God was being pushy!

I invited all those requesting prayer to come around the altar. I asked the folks to come close to the tabernacle. As Archbishop Fulton Sheen used to say, when you want to get warm, you come close to the fire; when you want to come close to our Lord Jesus, you approach the tabernacle.

I began the healing prayer by reminding the people about the great price that our Lord Jesus Christ had to pay so that we could be healed. In Isaiah 53:3-5, it is prophesied:

He was despised and forsaken by humans,
 a man of pains and knowing grief;
He was like one from whom people hide their faces.
 He was despised and we did not take him into account.

Surely, our diseases he bore
  and our pains he carried.
But we accounted him as one stricken,
  struck by God and afflicted.
And he was wounded for our rebelliousness,
  crushed because of our iniquities.
Correction for the sake of our health was upon him,
  and by his stripes we were healed.

Since the prophet Isaiah announces the power of the Messiah's suffering to heal and forgive us, and since the New Testament proclaims the fulfillment of this good news in Jesus Christ our Lord, then we ought to pray for healing with the power of Christ's suffering at the forefront of our thoughts. I began our prayer by asking the assembled brothers and sisters to bring to mind the suffering and passion of Christ our Lord. Then I prayed:

Lord, we praise you and bless you. You have held back no good thing from us. Father in heaven, you have even given us your own beloved Son, Jesus, our Lord. Lord Jesus, you gave us your own life so that we might be forgiven of all our sins and healed of our diseases and ailments. There is nothing in this creation that is stronger than the weakness of your death on the cross. We thank you for the salvation you have won for us.

When you went to the Garden of Gethsemane to pray, you so desired the comfort of God the Father and your friends. Like all of us, you did not desire to suffer pain. However, you were willing to accept the will of your Abba, even when it meant torture and death. By the power of your agony in the garden, heal all of us who have experienced the absence of consolation in prayer. Heal those who do not experience the comforting presence and peace of the Father when they try to listen to him. Strengthen those who hear only silence when they pray. Heal us by the power of your own agonized prayer.

You also were abandoned and betrayed by your closest friends in the garden. Your loyal disciples could not stay awake to pray with you. Judas betrayed you with a kiss; the other eleven ran away when the soldiers came to arrest you. Peter denied even knowing you when he was questioned by the servants of the high priest. You were left alone in your suffering. By your loneliness in this trial, heal all of us who are alone. Some of us have been abandoned by our husbands and wives through divorce. Some of us have been abandoned by our parents or our children or our brothers and sisters. Some have lost family and friends through death and feel all alone. Heal us of this loneliness by your aloneness in the garden and the high priest's court.

Lord, let the power of your suffering and death heal us now. It is by your stripes that we are healed. Therefore, let the stripes of your cruelly scourged flesh heal us. Your flesh was torn by the whips. Let this destruction of your skin heal all of our skin diseases. Heal those who have skin cancer, jaundice, psoriasis, and other skin disorders by the power of the ripping of your flesh.

When you were scourged, your flesh was so mutilated that your bones were exposed. "I can number all my bones"

(Psalm 22:18). Therefore, heal all those who have bone disorders. Heal those with broken bones; heal those with bone cancer and leukemia. Strengthen those with calcium deficiencies. Heal our bones by the power of the suffering that exposed your sacred bones through your scourging.

Heal also those who commit sins of the flesh. By the tearing of your flesh, heal those addicted to pornography and sexual sin. Heal those who eat so much as to harm their bodies with obesity. Let these and any other sins of the flesh be overcome by the power of the torment of your flesh during your scourging.

In order to make you look ridiculous and foolish, the soldiers crowned your head with thorns. This caused a double agony of humiliation and physical pain. Let this humiliation heal our memories of those times when we were mocked by other people. Help us to love those who ridicule us. By the crowning of thorns, forgive us of all of our vanity, pride, and arrogance. We sin against you by trying to make ourselves more than what we ought to be.

By the crowning of thorns, also heal us of any disorders of the head. Heal all tumors and cancers of the brain. Heal us of stroke and its effects. Heal those who have any mental problems. Heal all neurological disorders. Let us think thoughts that give you praise and glory. Fill our heads with your truth, for you are the truth (John 14:6).

When you walked the way of the cross, you had to bear its weight on your own back. Some of us feel as if we are carrying the weight of the world on our own shoulders. We feel as if we must do everything that needs to be done in the world. Heal us of those times when we take on too much work and too many burdens. Let us know that your yoke is easy and your burden light, since you are the one who carried the cross of our salvation.

Heal all those who suffer from various kinds of back pain. Heal those with slipped disks, broken backs, muscle strain, curvature of the spine, and dislocated shoulders. You bore our pains on your back on the way to Calvary; bear our pains still.

When you arrived at Calvary, you were stripped of your garments to be killed naked and poor, leaving this world just as you came into it. Heal those who suffer because of the shame of poverty. Heal those who feel shame for their own body with its physical limitations and even for its less beautiful elements. By the shame forced upon you, heal us of our shame.

You were attached to the cross by nails in your hands and your feet. Many of us feel trapped in our lives. We feel as if we cannot move from our present situation, and it seems that we have lost our freedom. Heal us of that sense of loss of freedom by your own loss of freedom to move when you were nailed to the cross and would not come down, despite the taunts of the enemies challenging you to do so.

Heal us of all disorders of the hands and feet. Keep us from stretching out our hands to work evil and from walking into sin. By your suffering keep us away from even those near occasions of sin that bring us to the brink of falling. Heal those who have disorders of the hands and feet. Especially heal those with arthritis and rheumatism.

Strengthen all our joints, and make us whole so that we may use our hands and feet to serve your people and to spread your good news of salvation.

When you hung upon the cross, you were offered wine in your dying moments. Many of us feel that without alcohol or drugs we would die because we are addicted to these substances. Heal us of our addictions to alcohol, cocaine, marijuana, or other drugs. Whether we are physically or psychologically dependent on these drugs, free us from them all. By the power of your death, liberate us from the fear of dying because of a lack of addicting substances.

As you hung upon the cross, the sky darkened and death drew near. Heal all of us who are dying at this time. Some of us have been told that medicine cannot heal us. Some of us know that our time of death is near and that death is certain, yet each moment goes slowly because this time of dying is without action to distract us. We feel as doomed as you felt hanging on the cross. Heal us of the fear of death by giving us the power to commend our spirits into the hands of the Father, just as you did. Give us the ability to see meaning in our lives and in our deaths by the power of your self-sacrifice on the cross. Let us know that by our sufferings, we make up for what is still lacking in your sufferings (Colossians 1:24) for the sake of your Mystical Body, the Church. Give us the ability to see that death leads to resurrection for those who have faith in your death and resurrection. Show us that death has meaning, and therefore life is worth living, not for ourselves, but for you and for your kingdom.

Heal us, Lord Jesus, of all our disorders. Heal us, not for the sake of our own fear or self-centeredness, but heal us for the greater praise and glory of our Father in heaven. Amen.

Any one of us can reflect on the individual events of Christ's passion and death, and then apply them to our own situations of pain and suffering. In this type of prayer, we can actively hear God the Father speaking to us because through Jesus, he has joined us in our human suffering and pain. Because he hears our suffering so profoundly, we can hear him speak to us in our suffering. Not only do we recognize God's sympathy with us, but we also can hear him speaking to us of the meaning and purpose of suffering.

As we learn to cope with the situation and perhaps even come to accept it, we begin to find a certain peace and even joy. Feeling God's peace does not mean that the pain of the situation goes away. Rather, we discover a new level of meaning within the pain. We can learn to unite our suffering with Christ's pain during his passion and death on the cross. This opens our minds and hearts to a new level of trust in God: He can bring good out of my problems, just as he brought salvation to the sinners of the world through Christ's death.

Suffering and Our Mission on Earth

We have already connected our own experience of suffering with that of Jeremiah, Jonah, and Jesus, especially in the case in which we suffer because of our faithfulness to God's call to us. However, there is still another level of meaning in these challenges and problems. Sometimes suffering is not only the result of being faithful to God's mission; sometimes pain actually becomes one of the means by which the mission is accomplished. Let's focus again on Jesus.

Jesus announced to his disciples, "For the Son of man also came not to be served but to serve, and to give his life as a ransom for many" (Mark 10:45). He said this after the third prediction of his passion. After each of these announcements, the disciples tried to talk him out of such a mission (8:32-33), or they changed the subject to a discussion about which of them was the greatest (9:34) or about which one could sit closest to him on his right and left (10:37-40). However, not only did Jesus know he was going to suffer and die, and not only did he continue to walk directly toward Jerusalem, the site of this suffering, but he saw it as his very mission and purpose.

The depths of this mystery are great, and a few reflections on the meaning of Jesus' mission would be appropriate here. First, remember that from the very beginning, death was the punishment for sin. "And the LORD God commanded the man, saying, 'You may freely eat of every tree of the garden; but of the tree of the knowledge of good and evil you shall not eat, for in the day that you eat of it you shall die'" (Genesis 2:16-17). The first Adam failed to keep the commandment, but the death penalty was delayed until he and his wife began the family of the human race. However, death came to all humanity. Jesus Christ, who committed no sin, died as an innocent "Lamb of God who takes away the sins of the world" (John 1:29). His death is the acceptance of a punishment due to sinners, which redeems them because the one who died did not deserve it. Furthermore, Jesus is God the Son—he is infinite, coequal with the Father and the Holy Spirit in divine essence. Precisely because he is God and man, he is an infinite sacrifice for sin. Not only was his death strong enough to take away the debt of punishment due to man's sin, but he is so truly infinite that he can take the punishment due to the sin of every human being that has ever been born or ever will be born. This infinity even means that no sin committed by mortal man can be more powerful than the death of God the Son on the cross. Each and every sin, no matter how heinous or shameful, can be forgiven. Therefore, by his suffering and death, Christ can reconcile everyone who believes in the power of that saving death, turns to him in faith, and asks for forgiveness for sins and reconciliation with God.

> Anytime we pray, we can make a spiritual offering of ourselves in union with Jesus Christ and his sufferings.

If the death of the completely innocent Jesus Christ, who is God made man, is inherently linked to his mission of salvation, then how can the suffering of Christians today be linked to their mission on earth?

First, the suffering we endure can be joined to that of Jesus' suffering, as the meditation here on the passion of Christ showed. In this we can find ourselves in the various aspects of Christ's suffering. Beyond that, we can also make our present difficulties and suffering into an offering to God when we unite them with those of Jesus Christ. St. Paul wrote: "I appeal to you therefore, brethren, by the mercies of God, to present your bodies as a living sacrifice, holy and acceptable to God, which is your spiritual worship" (Romans 12:1). This is not only an offering of our strengths and talents but also of our weaknesses and suffering. Anytime we pray, we can make a spiritual offering of ourselves in union with Jesus Christ and his sufferings.

However, the moment par excellence to make this sacrifice is at Mass. At the offertory we present gifts of bread and wine, and the priest lifts each gift as an offering of our human efforts to God. These are apt symbols of our suffering, since both wheat and grapes are crushed before becoming our offering. Then the wheat is baked and the grapes are fermented, processes which symbolize our own sufferings. More profound than the offering of these gifts is the consecration of them, where by the action of the Holy Spirit and the power of the words Jesus Christ gave us, the bread becomes the Body of Christ and the wine becomes his Blood. The consecration particularly symbolizes the death of Christ, since the separate consecration of Body and Blood symbolizes their separation at death. In this way, the natural gifts, including the sufferings we have offered, are not merely human efforts but are now consecrated and united to Jesus Christ on the cross. Jesus is the one who elevates what we have offered.

In the last great moment of the Mass, the priest always mixes a particle of the Body of Christ with his Blood in the chalice. This symbolizes Jesus' rising from the dead. Then the Body and Blood are consumed, also a sign of the resurrection. For all who receive Christ in the Eucharist, Communion offers the hope that their sufferings will be transformed as Jesus' sufferings were transformed in his resurrection. We have hope because Jesus' mission to suffer made possible the eternal life of the resurrection and opened the gates of heaven; we also have hope because our suffering will bring about a greater good than we can ever imagine. We may not know what that will be; we may not see the results in this life any more than the martyrs did, but we have a confidence anchored in the experience of Jesus' resurrection from the dead.

The Wounds of Christ Glorified

An important aspect of the resurrection is portrayed in the gospel reading on the Sunday after Easter, when the apostle Thomas doubts the resurrection. Appropriately enough, we usually focus on Thomas' doubts until he saw Christ, while Christ commends the greater blessing for those who have faith without having seen him (John 20:27-29). However, we often overlook the fact that Thomas was able to touch the wounds in Christ's hands, feet, and side (John 20:27). This means that the wounds of our Lord, risen from the dead, were glorified and still evident to the apostles. St. John also saw the glorified Christ in heaven as "a Lamb standing, as though it had been slain" (Revelation 5:6).

The glorification of Christ's wounds has at least two important ramifications. First, his wounds still maintain their power to heal, fulfilling the prophecy of Isaiah 53:5 ("By his stripes we were healed") for all time. Second, they provide a model for all the saints, living and dead. We can seek the intercession of the saints whose experiences resonate with our own precisely because they suffered. St. Rita is so popular with wives whose husbands are abusive because she offers the hope of their conversion. St. Elizabeth of Portugal suffered to have her warring sons become reconciled. St. Monica shed many tears and tremendous anxiety for her son, Augustine, who had strayed from his faith but eventually became a great priest, bishop, and theologian. Often we choose patron saints because they had the same struggles that we are also experiencing, and they found the grace to overcome them.

Our own struggles may seem overwhelming, embarrassing, and painful at the time we are going through them. We may simply wish they would be over. Yet precisely because we have joined them to the passion of Christ and have found his grace in overcoming the challenges and pain, we may end up seeing them as the most significant moments of our lives. We come to find the meaning of life in them because, like the wounds in Christ's hands and feet and side, our wounds become a witness to God's goodness and a source of strength to ourselves and to other people.

I look back on my personal experiences with the New Age movement in the early 1970s as an embarrassing set of episodes in which I held some dumb and even sinful ideas. However, after a few years of being free from New Age teachings, I was able to write a book about its foibles and traps, based on my own experiences and research. I thank our Lord that my having given up folly has become a vehicle for helping others get out of it.

As a newly ordained priest, I visited a brother Jesuit in the hospital. He was dying of cancer after many years of being a recovered alcoholic and a successful alcoholism counselor. His last words to me were these: "The best thing that ever happened to me is that I became an alcoholic. If I had not, I would have stayed too arrogant to be good for God or for anyone else. I would never have met other alcoholics and learned about life from them." Many other recovering alcoholics and drug addicts have echoed this sentiment. Their deadly weakness so humbled them that they had no one else to turn to but God. They found him and were converted by their weaknesses and their need for his strength.

These stories highlight the fact that suffering endured in Christ and for Christ becomes linked with our missions in life. Suffering was inherent to Christ's mission (Mark 10:45). So also those Christians who join their sufferings with his will discover that their suffering is tied intimately with their mission in the world. The witness of martyrs has often converted people on the spot. Perhaps we will never face martyrdom, but we have our own

> Suffering endured in Christ and for Christ becomes linked with our missions in life.

struggles that belong to our mission in life. The parents who lovingly lose sleep over a sick child, or the elderly spouse who takes care of a lifelong companion, have their own particular trials to endure. At times the trials are the essence of the mission to live in a family, along with all the joys and benefits. They are never signs of failure but an aspect of the mission that is as linked to Christ's cross as the stones that were thrown at St. Stephen, the very first martyr. We can eventually rejoice in them as we find foretastes of Christ's resurrection. That may occur immediately, or it may be delayed until the experience becomes more fully integrated. Yet through it all, we can learn to listen to God's powerful voice and hear him speak lovingly, even when we hurt. Our Savior Jesus accomplished his mission in such a way, and we, his disciples in the modern world, can learn to do the same.

Questions for Reflection and Discussion

1. Do you expect God to take away your pain when you pray to him? How can we see difficulties as opportunities for God to speak to us in a new way?

2. When have you seen God bring good out of some pain or difficulty you were undergoing? How did this increase your trust in him?

3. What Scripture passages have spoken to you in difficult times? Think of someone you know who is suffering. How could you share with that person the comfort and strength that you have received from God's word?

4. Have you ever connected your suffering with your mission on earth? How might your experiences help others?

5. Which saints have most influenced your life and why? How do the lives and the intercession of the saints give you hope that your sufferings will be transformed?

CONCLUSION

THE END GAME

We've made the decision to listen to God. We're communicating with him each day in prayer, attentive to the movements in our souls. We employ our intellect, our will, and our emotions. Now what? What's our goal? What's the "end point"?

We can expect that the more we make an effort to listen to God, the more he will move and form us. The basic principles enunciated in the first chapters of this book and in St. Ignatius' Rules for the Discernment of Spirits are absolutely important directives for learning to listen. However, the experience of prayer, whether personal or communal, and the experience of trying to discern God's will in concrete circumstances and crises of life will shape our personalities. We should expect to become more easily attuned to God's presence and absence, the peace or lack thereof by which we discern his will.

We can expect to become more sensitive to the objective truths revealed in Scripture. The longer we obey God's commandments, the more deeply we learn from our mistakes in disobeying them and the more we understand the purpose of these laws. We come to appreciate the eternal majesty of God and the inherent dignity of each person who is created in his image and likeness. We become more sensitive to God's values as we live them, and our relationships with God and our fellow human beings become much richer and more peaceful than they were before we took God so seriously.

Daily we become more sensitive to the purpose of prayer and listening to God. Therefore, listening to God in prayer needs to be a component of life woven into each day. Each day we will find new challenges in raising children or in relating to a spouse. Each day we will find people who need to hear the good news of salvation. Each day we will meet fellow Christians who are struggling to keep their faith or maintain their moral uprightness. Each day we will confront various crises, and we will need to respond to them. Daily we may encounter our own larger and lesser failures and frustrations. Therefore, we need to pray and listen to God daily. In this way we can integrate the life of faith with every other component of our human existence, whether physical, emotional, spiritual, or social. The ongoing experiences of life will be integrated by the presence and actions of God, and we become far better men and women because of that.

Another purpose of listening to God is to follow his lead, trust in his providence, and then watch how he acts to save us with various signs and wonders. These experiences of God's actions are sometimes small and sometimes large, and we experience a joy that overflows when we witness them. We respond by giving him thanks and praise for all that he does. Our praise, honor, and glory satisfy the deepest desires of our heart and the very purpose for which we were created. That joy cannot be found in such depth apart from sharing the adventure of letting God act powerfully in our lives and then thanking him for it.

Is death the end of listening to God? Maybe. If we die unrepentant and separated from God, we will be unable to listen to God. No one hears him in hell.

But maybe not. In heaven we will see God face-to-face. We will be able to listen to him directly and with new understanding. Then listening will take place on a whole new level. I suspect that the things we have heard from God in this life will be akin to the sounds of a symphony orchestra tuning up their instruments. When we see him in heaven, the symphony will begin in earnest, with a harmony beyond all imagination, satisfying the soul and mind beyond anything we could have hoped for. In heaven, the listening will truly begin.

the WORD
among us ®
The *Spirit* of Catholic Living

This book was published by The Word Among Us. Since 1981, The Word Among Us has been answering the call of the Second Vatican Council to help Catholic laypeople encounter Christ in the Scriptures.

The name of our company comes from the prologue to the Gospel of John and reflects the vision and purpose of all of our publications: to be an instrument of the Spirit, whose desire is to manifest Jesus' presence in and to the children of God. In this way, we hope to contribute to the Church's ongoing mission of proclaiming the gospel to the world so that all people would know the love and mercy of our Lord and grow ever more deeply in love with him.

Our monthly devotional magazine, *The Word Among Us*, features meditations on the daily and Sunday Mass readings, and currently reaches more than one million Catholics in North America and another half million Catholics in one hundred countries around the world. Our book division, The Word Among Us Press, publishes numerous books, Bible studies, and pamphlets that help Catholics grow in their faith.

To learn more about who we are and what we publish, log on to our website at www.wau.org. There you will find a variety of Catholic resources that will help you grow in your faith.

Embrace His Word, Listen to God . . .

www.wau.org